GitHub Copilot Cer

Practice Questions

Copyright © 2025 by GitHub Copilot Certification
All rights reserved.
No part of this book may be reproduced, distributed, or transmitted in any form or by any
means, including photocopying, recording, or other electronic or mechanical methods, without
the prior written permission of the publisher, except in the case of brief quotations embodied
in critical reviews and certain other noncommercial uses permitted by copyright law.

Table of Contents

About GitHub Copilot Certification

Introduction

GitHub Copilot is revolutionizing the way developers write code by leveraging AI-powered assistance to generate code, suggest improvements, and enhance productivity. As software development becomes increasingly complex, tools like GitHub Copilot enable developers to focus on solving problems rather than getting bogged down by repetitive coding tasks. By integrating seamlessly into popular Integrated Development Environments (IDEs), GitHub Copilot accelerates development workflows and helps teams deliver high-quality software faster.

The **GitHub Copilot Certification** is designed to equip professionals with the skills needed to maximize the potential of this cutting-edge AI assistant. Whether you are a new developer looking to improve your productivity, an experienced engineer seeking to streamline workflows, or a technical leader aiming to integrate AI into your development practices, this certification provides the knowledge and hands-on expertise to succeed in today's AI-enhanced development landscape.

Why Learn GitHub Copilot?

GitHub Copilot is transforming the way developers approach coding. By providing real-time suggestions, auto-generating boilerplate code, and assisting in debugging, Copilot allows developers to focus on creativity and problem-solving. Mastering GitHub Copilot empowers you to:

- **Boost Productivity**: Automate repetitive coding tasks and reduce time spent writing boilerplate code.

- **Write Better Code**: Leverage AI suggestions for cleaner, optimized, and bug-free implementations.
- **Learn Faster**: Discover new programming languages, frameworks, and best practices with Copilot's contextual assistance.
- **Enhance Collaboration**: Work more effectively in teams by standardizing coding styles and improving code quality.

As organizations adopt AI-first development strategies, gaining expertise with GitHub Copilot can set you apart in the job market and help you deliver high-quality software efficiently. This certification ensures you are equipped to utilize Copilot effectively, whether for personal projects, open-source contributions, or professional software development.

Who Should Take This Certification?

The GitHub Copilot Certification is suitable for a wide range of learners, regardless of their experience level in software development or AI tools. This certification is ideal for:

- **Beginner Developers**: Learn how to code faster and more effectively with Copilot's assistance, even as you explore new programming languages and frameworks.
- **Experienced Developers**: Streamline workflows, reduce errors, and adopt AI-driven development practices to improve productivity.
- **Open-Source Contributors**: Leverage Copilot to make meaningful contributions to open-source projects with clean, consistent, and high-quality code.
- **Team Leads and Technical Managers**: Understand how Copilot can enhance team collaboration, accelerate development cycles, and improve code consistency across projects.

What You'll Learn

This certification includes a comprehensive curriculum covering all aspects of GitHub Copilot, from foundational concepts to advanced techniques. Here's an overview of the key learning outcomes:

1. GitHub Copilot Basics

Learn how to integrate GitHub Copilot into your favorite development environment, including Visual Studio Code, JetBrains IDEs, and more. Explore how Copilot generates suggestions, completes code, and provides real-time assistance.

- Setting up GitHub Copilot in your IDE
- Understanding AI-powered code generation
- Leveraging Copilot for code completion and debugging

2. Writing Code with Copilot

Discover how to use Copilot effectively for different programming paradigms and languages, including object-oriented, functional, and procedural programming.

- Generating boilerplate code for faster development
- Writing tests with Copilot's assistance
- Debugging and refactoring with AI suggestions

3. Open-Source Contributions with Copilot

Learn how to use Copilot to contribute to open-source projects effectively. This module covers best practices for writing clean, maintainable code and adhering to project-specific guidelines.

- Using Copilot for documentation and code consistency
- Navigating legacy and poorly documented codebases with AI assistance
- Collaborating with other contributors using AI-driven tools

4. Advanced Techniques with GitHub Copilot

Explore advanced features of Copilot, including writing complex algorithms, integrating DevOps workflows, and troubleshooting limitations in AI-generated code.

- Customizing Copilot suggestions with contextual comments
- Automating repetitive coding tasks
- Addressing Copilot's limitations in edge cases

Hands-On Labs & Practical Experience

This certification emphasizes practical learning through hands-on labs and real-world scenarios. Participants will work on projects that allow them to:

- Automate repetitive tasks with Copilot
- Write clean, optimized code in multiple languages
- Debug and refactor legacy codebases with Copilot's assistance
- Contribute to open-source projects using AI tools

By the end of this certification, you'll have practical experience applying GitHub Copilot to real-world development tasks, ensuring you can use the tool effectively in professional settings.

Certification Exam Details

To earn the GitHub Copilot Certification, you must pass an exam that evaluates your understanding of Copilot features and your ability to use them effectively in development workflows. Below are the exam details:

- **Number of Questions**: 50
- **Duration**: 90 minutes
- **Passing Score**: 70% (35 correct answers)
- **Exam Format**: Multiple-choice and scenario-based questions
- **Practice Exam**: Included in the course to help you prepare

The Growing Demand for This Certification

As AI-driven development tools like GitHub Copilot become mainstream, developers with expertise in using these tools effectively are in high demand. The benefits of mastering Copilot include:

- **Increased Productivity**: Accelerate coding workflows and deliver projects faster.
- **Improved Code Quality**: Write cleaner, more maintainable, and error-free code.
- **Career Advancement**: Gain a competitive edge in the job market by demonstrating expertise in AI-assisted development.

The global software development industry is rapidly adopting AI tools, and professionals with GitHub Copilot expertise are becoming indispensable for modern development teams.

Job Opportunities After This Certification

Earning the GitHub Copilot Certification can open doors to various roles in the software development and AI-driven technology space, such as:

- **Software Developer** – Leverage Copilot to write clean, efficient code.
- **DevOps Engineer** – Automate workflows and enhance CI/CD pipelines with AI tools.
- **Open-Source Contributor** – Contribute high-quality, maintainable code to community projects.
- **Technical Lead** – Improve team productivity and code consistency with Copilot.
- **AI Integration Specialist** – Build AI-driven development workflows and tools.

With this certification, you'll be equipped with the skills to excel in an AI-enhanced development environment and make significant contributions to your organization.

Practice Questions with Answers

Domain 1: Introduction to GitHub Copilot

1. What type of tasks can GitHub Copilot assist with?

A) Writing code, debugging, and generating documentation.

B) Managing cloud infrastructure.

C) Performing automated deployments.

D) Replacing manual code reviews.

Answer: A

Explanation: GitHub Copilot assists with writing code, debugging, and generating documentation, making development more efficient.

2. How does GitHub Copilot use machine learning models?

A) It uses pre-trained models to generate code suggestions based on context and comments.

B) It trains new models for every project.

C) It uses static rules for generating suggestions.

D) It does not use machine learning models.

Answer: A

Explanation: GitHub Copilot uses pre-trained machine learning models to generate context-aware code suggestions.

3. What is a limitation of GitHub Copilot regarding proprietary code?

A) It can only suggest open-source code.

B) It may inadvertently suggest code snippets that resemble proprietary code.

C) It cannot work with private repositories.

D) It requires explicit approval for using proprietary code.

Answer: B

Explanation: GitHub Copilot may inadvertently suggest code snippets that resemble proprietary code, so developers need to review suggested code carefully.

4. Which IDEs are supported by GitHub Copilot?

A) Visual Studio Code, JetBrains IDEs, and Neovim.

B) Only Visual Studio Code.

C) Sublime Text and Atom.

D) Eclipse and NetBeans.

Answer: A

Explanation: GitHub Copilot supports Visual Studio Code, JetBrains IDEs, and Neovim.

5. How does GitHub Copilot generate context-aware suggestions?

A) By analyzing the entire project codebase.

B) By using comments and the surrounding code as inputs.

C) By reviewing external documentation.

D) By downloading external libraries dynamically.

Answer: B

Explanation: GitHub Copilot generates context-aware suggestions by using comments and the surrounding code as inputs.

6. What is the primary benefit of GitHub Copilot Chat?

A) It provides real-time collaboration with other developers.

B) It allows developers to ask questions about code and get AI-generated explanations.

C) It automatically generates unit tests for all functions.

D) It handles project management tasks.

Answer: B

Explanation: GitHub Copilot Chat allows developers to ask questions about code and get AI-generated explanations, helping them understand the codebase faster.

7. What is GitHub's approach to protecting sensitive information with Copilot?

A) By encrypting all communications between the IDE and GitHub servers.

B) By ignoring code that contains sensitive information like API keys.

C) By only training models on publicly available data.

D) By not allowing Copilot to function in private repositories.

Answer: B

Explanation: GitHub Copilot protects sensitive information by ignoring code that contains sensitive information like API keys.

8. How can GitHub Copilot help with learning new programming languages?

A) By providing tutorials within the IDE.

B) By suggesting code snippets and examples in the language being used.

C) By generating a complete project in the new language.

D) By running automated code translations.

Answer: B

Explanation: GitHub Copilot helps with learning new programming languages by suggesting code snippets and examples in the language being used.

9. What is a best practice when using GitHub Copilot for large projects?

A) Use Copilot suggestions without reviewing them.

B) Break down tasks into smaller pieces and provide clear comments.

C) Avoid using Copilot for complex code.

D) Only use Copilot for debugging.

Answer: B

Explanation: For large projects, it is best to break down tasks into smaller pieces and provide clear comments to get better suggestions from Copilot.

10. Which feature of GitHub Copilot is designed for teams and

organizations?

A) GitHub Copilot Chat.

B) GitHub Copilot Enterprise.

C) GitHub Copilot Individuals.

D) Copilot Terminal Assistant.

Answer: B

Explanation: GitHub Copilot Enterprise is designed for teams and organizations, offering features like prompt and suggestion collection.

11. What is the role of comments in enhancing GitHub Copilot's suggestions?

A) Comments are ignored by GitHub Copilot.

B) Comments provide context, helping Copilot generate more accurate suggestions.

C) Comments are used to generate documentation.

D) Comments disable Copilot suggestions.

Answer: B

Explanation: Comments provide context, helping Copilot generate more accurate suggestions tailored to the specific task.

12. How can GitHub Copilot improve collaboration in a team?

A) By replacing team discussions with AI-generated solutions.

B) By providing shared suggestions and context-aware code for the entire team.

C) By creating automated pull requests.

D) By assigning tasks to team members.

Answer: B

Explanation: GitHub Copilot improves collaboration by providing shared suggestions and context-aware code for the entire team.

13. What is the purpose of GitHub Copilot Labs?

A) To provide early access to experimental features for developers.

B) To replace GitHub Copilot entirely.

C) To manage repositories more efficiently.

D) To automate DevOps pipelines.

Answer: A

Explanation: GitHub Copilot Labs provides early access to experimental features for developers.

14. How does GitHub Copilot handle multi-language projects?

A) It works only with the primary language of the project.

B) It understands and provides suggestions for all supported languages in the project.

C) It requires separate configurations for each language.

D) It ignores non-primary languages.

Answer: B

Explanation: GitHub Copilot understands and provides suggestions for all supported languages in a multi-language project.

15. What is a key limitation of GitHub Copilot when working with legacy codebases?

A) Copilot cannot analyze legacy codebases.

B) Copilot may have difficulty understanding complex or poorly documented legacy code.

C) Copilot does not support older programming languages.

D) Copilot requires internet access for legacy codebases.

Answer: B

Explanation: GitHub Copilot may have difficulty understanding complex or poorly documented legacy code.

16. Which programming paradigms does GitHub Copilot support?

A) Only object-oriented programming.

B) Only functional programming.

C) All major programming paradigms, including object-oriented and functional.

D) Only procedural programming.

Answer: C

Explanation: GitHub Copilot supports all major programming paradigms, including object-oriented and functional programming.

17. What is one way GitHub Copilot can assist with documentation?

A) By automatically publishing documentation to GitHub Pages.

B) By generating comments and docstrings based on code.

C) By creating a detailed project report.

D) By converting code into plain text.

Answer: B

Explanation: GitHub Copilot can assist with documentation by generating comments and docstrings based on code.

18. How can developers ensure GitHub Copilot generates secure code?

A) By only using it for open-source projects.

B) By reviewing all suggestions and testing the code for vulnerabilities.

C) By enabling the "secure mode" in their IDE.

D) By relying entirely on Copilot's built-in security features.

Answer: B

Explanation: Developers should review all suggestions and test the code for vulnerabilities to ensure it is secure.

19. What is the significance of the GitHub Copilot Code of Conduct?

A) It provides guidelines for ethical and responsible use of GitHub Copilot.

B) It restricts access to GitHub Copilot for non-developers.

C) It enforces a specific coding style for all users.

D) It limits the use of Copilot to certain programming languages.

Answer: A

Explanation: The GitHub Copilot Code of Conduct provides guidelines for ethical and responsible use of GitHub Copilot.

20. How does GitHub Copilot benefit open-source contributors?

A) By automating the submission of pull requests.

B) By increasing productivity and reducing development time.

C) By replacing the need for code reviews.

D) By generating licenses for open-source projects.

Answer: B

Explanation: GitHub Copilot benefits open-source contributors by increasing productivity and reducing development time.

21. Which GitHub Copilot plan is best suited for a large multinational corporation with high security and compliance needs, including support for SSO and audit logs?

A) Copilot Individual

B) Copilot Business

C) Copilot Enterprise

D) Copilot Business for non-GHE

Answer: C

Explanation: Copilot Enterprise is tailored for organizations with rigorous security and compliance requirements, offering features like Single Sign-On (SSO), audit logs, and support for both cloud-hosted and self-hosted environments.

22. What feature of GitHub Copilot Enterprise supports advanced authentication methods?

A) GitHub Codespaces

B) Single Sign-On (SSO)

C) Multi-language support

D) Automated unit test generation

Answer: B

Explanation: Single Sign-On (SSO) provides advanced authentication methods, ensuring secure access for enterprise users.

23. Why is Copilot Business not ideal for a multinational corporation with self-hosted environments?

A) It lacks support for cloud-hosted environments.

B) It does not include advanced security features like SSO and audit logs.

C) It only supports freelance developers.

D) It does not allow multiple users.

Answer: B

Explanation: Copilot Business lacks advanced security features like SSO and audit logs, which are essential for multinational corporations with self-hosted environments.

24. Which plan is designed for freelance developers or individual users?

A) Copilot Individual

B) Copilot Business

C) Copilot Enterprise

D) Copilot Business for non-GHE

Answer: A

Explanation: Copilot Individual is designed for freelance developers or individual users.

25. What is a key benefit of GitHub Copilot for enterprise teams?

A) Automated deployment workflows.

B) Context-aware code suggestions.

C) Built-in project management tools.

D) Automated bug fixes.

Answer: B

Explanation: GitHub Copilot provides context-aware code suggestions, which help enterprise teams improve productivity and reduce development time.

26. How does GitHub Copilot assist with understanding existing codebases?

A) By running automated tests.

B) By generating visual diagrams of code structures.

C) By answering questions and providing explanations through GitHub Copilot Chat.

D) By automatically refactoring code.

Answer: C

Explanation: GitHub Copilot Chat helps developers understand existing codebases by answering questions and providing explanations.

27. Which GitHub Copilot plan supports both cloud-hosted and on-

premise environments?

A) Copilot Individual

B) Copilot Business

C) Copilot Enterprise

D) Copilot Business for non-GHE

Answer: C

Explanation: Copilot Enterprise supports both cloud-hosted and on-premise environments, making it ideal for organizations with diverse operational needs.

28. What feature ensures regulatory compliance for enterprises using GitHub Copilot?

A) Multi-language support.

B) Detailed audit logs.

C) Automated code completion.

D) GitHub Codespaces.

Answer: B

Explanation: Detailed audit logs ensure regulatory compliance by providing a record of actions taken within GitHub Copilot.

29. How can GitHub Copilot help developers write secure code?

A) By storing passwords in the codebase.

B) By suggesting secure coding practices and ignoring sensitive information like API keys.

C) By automatically encrypting all code.

D) By replacing developers.

Answer: B

Explanation: GitHub Copilot helps developers write secure code by suggesting secure coding practices and ignoring sensitive information like API keys.

30. Why is SSO important for enterprise users of GitHub Copilot?

A) It enables automated pull requests.

B) It provides a secure method for user authentication.

C) It allows anonymous access to repositories.

D) It helps in debugging code.

Answer: B

Explanation: Single Sign-On (SSO) provides a secure method for user authentication, which is crucial for enterprise users.

31. What is the main focus of GitHub Copilot Enterprise?

A) Individual productivity.

B) Advanced security and compliance.

C) Automated deployments.

D) Code refactoring.

Answer: B

Explanation: GitHub Copilot Enterprise focuses on advanced security and compliance for organizational needs.

32. How does GitHub Copilot improve developer productivity?

A) By automating all deployments.

B) By suggesting code snippets and solutions in real-time.

C) By replacing developers in the coding process.

D) By managing repositories.

Answer: B

Explanation: GitHub Copilot improves productivity by suggesting code snippets and solutions in real-time.

33. Which plan is best for small-to-medium-sized businesses that do not require self-hosted environments?

A) Copilot Individual

B) Copilot Business

C) Copilot Enterprise

D) Copilot for Open Source

Answer: B

Explanation: Copilot Business is ideal for small-to-medium-sized businesses that do not require self-hosted environments.

34. What is a limitation of GitHub Copilot Individual?

A) It does not support freelancers.

B) It lacks enterprise-level features like SSO and audit logs.

C) It only works with open-source projects.

D) It cannot be used for personal projects.

Answer: B

Explanation: GitHub Copilot Individual lacks enterprise-level features like SSO and audit logs.

35. What is one way GitHub Copilot ensures data privacy?

A) By encrypting all code it generates.

B) By anonymizing data sent to its AI model.

C) By storing all data locally.

D) By disabling internet access.

Answer: B

Explanation: GitHub Copilot ensures data privacy by anonymizing data sent to its AI model.

36. Which GitHub Copilot feature helps developers understand complex code?

A) GitHub Copilot Chat.

B) GitHub Actions.

C) GitHub Codespaces.

D) GitHub Audit Logs.

Answer: A

Explanation: GitHub Copilot Chat helps developers understand complex code by answering questions and providing explanations.

37. How does GitHub Copilot handle sensitive information in code?

A) By ignoring it during suggestion generation.

B) By encrypting all suggestions.

C) By storing it securely in the cloud.

D) By flagging it as a security issue.

Answer: A

Explanation: GitHub Copilot ignores sensitive information like API keys during suggestion generation to ensure security.

38. What is a best practice for using GitHub Copilot for large projects?

A) Use it without reviewing suggestions.

B) Provide clear comments and context to improve suggestion accuracy.

C) Avoid using it for complex tasks.

D) Only use it for debugging.

Answer: B

Explanation: Providing clear comments and context helps GitHub Copilot generate more accurate suggestions for large projects.

40. How can GitHub Copilot help developers learn a new programming language?

A) By providing tutorials.

B) By suggesting code snippets and examples in the language.

C) By offering online classes.

D) By automatically generating entire projects.

Answer: B

Explanation: GitHub Copilot helps developers learn a new programming language by suggesting code snippets and examples.

41. What is a key limitation of GitHub Copilot when working with legacy codebases?

A) Copilot cannot analyze legacy code.

B) Copilot may have difficulty understanding poorly documented legacy code.

C) Copilot does not support older programming languages.

D) Copilot requires internet access for legacy codebases.

Answer: B

Explanation: GitHub Copilot may have difficulty understanding poorly documented legacy code.

42. How can developers provide feedback on GitHub Copilot suggestions?

A) By using the feedback option in their IDE.

B) By submitting an issue on GitHub.

C) By modifying the suggestions and saving the file.

D) By emailing GitHub support.

Answer: A

Explanation: Developers can provide feedback on GitHub Copilot suggestions by using the feedback option in their IDE.

43. What is the primary focus of GitHub Copilot Chat?

A) Generating project documentation.

B) Answering questions about code and providing explanations.

C) Managing repositories.

D) Automating unit tests.

Answer: B

Explanation: GitHub Copilot Chat focuses on answering questions about code and providing explanations.

44. What type of projects is GitHub Copilot Individual best suited for?

A) Large enterprise projects.

B) Open-source and personal projects.

C) Legacy codebases.

D) Multi-language projects in enterprises.

Answer: B

Explanation: GitHub Copilot Individual is best suited for open-source and personal projects.

45. How does GitHub Copilot Enterprise support compliance?

A) By generating compliant code.

B) By providing detailed audit logs and SSO integration.

C) By automating compliance testing.

D) By restricting access to certain languages.

Answer: B

Explanation: GitHub Copilot Enterprise supports compliance by providing detailed audit logs and SSO integration.

46. Which IDEs are supported by GitHub Copilot?

A) Visual Studio Code, JetBrains IDEs, and Neovim.

B) Only Visual Studio Code.

C) Sublime Text and Atom.

D) Eclipse and NetBeans.

Answer: A

Explanation: GitHub Copilot supports Visual Studio Code, JetBrains IDEs, and Neovim.

47. What is the purpose of GitHub Copilot Labs?

A) To provide early access to experimental features for developers.

B) To replace GitHub Copilot entirely.

C) To manage repositories more efficiently.

D) To automate DevOps pipelines.

Answer: A

Explanation: GitHub Copilot Labs provides early access to experimental features for developers.

48. How does GitHub Copilot handle multi-language projects?

A) It works only with the primary language of the project.

B) It understands and provides suggestions for all supported languages in the project.

C) It requires separate configurations for each language.

D) It ignores non-primary languages.

Answer: B

Explanation: GitHub Copilot understands and provides suggestions for all supported languages in a multi-language project.

49. What is a key benefit of GitHub Copilot for open-source contributors?

A) Automating pull requests.

B) Increasing productivity by suggesting code snippets and solutions.

C) Replacing the need for code reviews.

D) Generating licenses for open-source projects.

Answer: B

Explanation: GitHub Copilot benefits open-source contributors by increasing productivity and reducing development time.

50. What is GitHub Copilot's primary focus for developers?

A) Automating deployments.

B) Enhancing productivity by providing AI-based code suggestions.

C) Replacing manual testing.

D) Managing GitHub repositories.

Answer: B

Explanation: GitHub Copilot's primary focus for developers is enhancing productivity by providing AI-based code suggestions.

51. Which GitHub Copilot plan is ideal for individual developers or freelancers?

A) Copilot Business

B) Copilot Individual

C) Copilot Enterprise

D) Copilot for Open Source

Answer: B

Explanation: Copilot Individual is designed for single users, like freelancers or independent developers, who want AI-powered coding assistance without enterprise-level features. It's a cost-effective solution for personal projects and learning. This plan does not include team collaboration tools.

52. What role does GitHub Copilot play in code reviews?

A) Automates the entire review process.

B) Provides code suggestions to reduce errors before a review.

C) Flags all issues in a pull request.

D) Generates automated documentation for reviews.

Answer: B

Explanation: GitHub Copilot assists developers by suggesting code improvements, reducing errors and improving code quality before reviews. It complements rather than replaces manual review processes. This ensures a higher standard of code submission. It does not automate the entire review process.

53. What is required to authenticate GitHub Copilot in any supported IDE?

A) A private repository token

B) A GitHub account

C) A third-party plugin

D) An SSH key

Answer: B

Explanation: A GitHub account is required to authenticate GitHub Copilot in supported IDEs. The account ensures access to the subscription and enables the AI to function seamlessly. Private tokens or SSH keys are not needed for basic authentication. This simplifies the setup process.

54. Which of the following is NOT a feature of GitHub Copilot?

A) Real-time code suggestions

B) Automated testing tools

C) Context-aware assistance

D) Multi-language support

Answer: B

Explanation: GitHub Copilot does not provide automated testing tools but can assist in generating unit test code. Its primary features include real-time suggestions, context-aware assistance, and multi-language support. Developers still need separate tools for automated testing processes.

55. How does GitHub Copilot help with debugging?

A) By automatically fixing bugs in code.

B) By suggesting fixes and improvements in real-time.

C) By running automated debug scripts.

D) By providing stack traces for errors.

Answer: B

Explanation: GitHub Copilot assists in debugging by suggesting fixes and improvements based on the context of the code. It does not automatically fix bugs or run debug scripts but enhances the developer's workflow. Debugging still requires developer oversight and validation.

56. Which programming languages are supported by GitHub Copilot?

A) Only JavaScript, Python, and Java

B) All major programming languages

C) Low-level languages only

D) Web-based languages only

Answer: B

Explanation: GitHub Copilot supports all major programming languages, including Python, JavaScript, Java, C++, and many more. Its versatility allows developers to work across various domains. This makes it suitable for both front-end and back-end development.

57. How does GitHub Copilot improve productivity for software teams?

A) By replacing team members with AI.

B) By automating the entire development process.

C) By providing faster, real-time suggestions and reducing repetitive coding tasks.

D) By generating project roadmaps.

Answer: C

Explanation: GitHub Copilot improves productivity by providing faster suggestions and reducing repetitive tasks. It allows developers to focus on higher-value aspects of the project. It complements team efforts rather than replacing them. Project management is outside its scope.

58. What is the first step to set up GitHub Copilot in JetBrains IDEs?

A) Enable GitHub Actions.

B) Install the GitHub Copilot plugin from the JetBrains marketplace.

C) Create a GitHub repository.

D) Enable Copilot in the JetBrains settings panel.

Answer: B

Explanation: The first step to set up GitHub Copilot in JetBrains IDEs is to install the Copilot plugin from the JetBrains marketplace. This provides seamless integration with IDEs like IntelliJ IDEA. Additional configuration can be done after installation.

59. Which of the following is a key advantage of GitHub Copilot for learning to code?

A) It eliminates the need for formal education.

B) It provides real-time examples and context-aware guidance.

C) It replaces coding instructors.

D) It generates entire projects automatically.

Answer: B

Explanation: GitHub Copilot helps learners by providing real-time examples and context-aware guidance, making it easier to understand new programming concepts. While it doesn't replace formal education or instructors, it acts as a valuable supplementary tool for learning.

60. What is the function of GitHub Copilot in Neovim?

A) Automating deployments

B) Providing AI-powered code suggestions directly in the editor

C) Managing GitHub repositories

D) Running shell scripts

Answer: B

Explanation: GitHub Copilot integrates with Neovim to provide AI-powered code suggestions directly in the editor. This enhances developer productivity by reducing time spent on repetitive coding tasks. It does not manage repositories or automate deployments.

61. What is a limitation of GitHub Copilot when working with private repositories?

A) It cannot be used in private repositories.

B) It requires explicit permission to access private repositories.

C) It only supports read-only access.

D) It automatically uploads private code to the cloud.

Answer: B

Explanation: GitHub Copilot requires explicit permission to access private repositories, ensuring data privacy and security. This gives developers control over what data is shared with the AI. It does not upload private code without authorization.

62. What is the primary purpose of GitHub Copilot's context-awareness?

A) To remember past projects.

B) To provide precise and relevant suggestions based on the surrounding code.

C) To store user-specific preferences.

D) To automate the entire development process.

Answer: B

Explanation: GitHub Copilot's context-awareness allows it to provide precise and relevant suggestions based on the surrounding code. This makes it an effective tool for writing, debugging, and learning code. It does not store past user projects or automate end-to-end development.

63. Which type of projects benefit most from GitHub Copilot's assistance?

A) Legacy projects only

B) Small, repetitive coding tasks and large-scale projects

C) Only cloud-based projects

D) AI-specific projects

Answer: B

Explanation: GitHub Copilot is useful for both small, repetitive coding tasks and large-scale projects, where it enhances productivity by providing intelligent suggestions. Its versatility makes it suitable for varied use cases. It is not limited to legacy or AI-specific projects.

64. Which type of subscription is required for accessing GitHub Copilot's full functionality?

A) Free GitHub account

B) GitHub Copilot subscription (Individual, Business, or Enterprise)

C) GitHub Actions subscription

D) GitHub CLI subscription

Answer: B

Explanation: To access GitHub Copilot's full functionality, a subscription (Individual, Business, or Enterprise) is required. Free GitHub accounts can only try Copilot in limited trial capacities. Paid subscriptions unlock advanced features and long-term usage.

65. What is the primary benefit of GitHub Copilot for experienced developers?

A) Eliminates the need for debugging.

B) Provides assistance in repetitive and boilerplate code tasks.

C) Replaces the need for team collaboration.

D) Automates deployment pipelines.

Answer: B

Explanation: Experienced developers benefit from GitHub Copilot by reducing the time spent on repetitive tasks and boilerplate code. This allows them to focus on solving complex problems. It does not replace debugging or collaboration but enhances productivity.

66. Which of the following commands can be used to install the GitHub

Copilot extension in Visual Studio Code?

A) npm install github-copilot

B) code --install-extension github.copilot

C) pip install github-copilot

D) apt-get install copilot

Answer: B

Explanation: The command code --install-extension github.copilot installs the GitHub Copilot extension in Visual Studio Code. This command is executed in the terminal. It is specific to the VS Code environment to ensure proper integration.

67. How does GitHub Copilot handle multi-language codebases?

A) It only supports the primary language in the project.

B) It can provide suggestions for all supported languages in the codebase.

C) It disables functionality for multi-language codebases.

D) It requires a separate Copilot instance for each language.

Answer: B

Explanation: GitHub Copilot provides suggestions for all supported languages in a multi-language codebase. This makes it versatile for projects involving multiple technologies. Developers can seamlessly switch between languages without reconfiguring Copilot.

68. Which of the following is a prerequisite for using GitHub Copilot in Neovim?

A) Installing a Copilot plugin for Neovim

B) Using a GitHub Enterprise account

C) Configuring SSH for GitHub Copilot

D) Enabling GitHub Actions

Answer: A

Explanation: To use GitHub Copilot in Neovim, developers must install a Copilot plugin for Neovim. This ensures proper integration into the editor. SSH and GitHub Actions are unrelated to Copilot's functionality in Neovim.

69. What is the role of machine learning in GitHub Copilot's functionality?

A) It enforces strict coding standards.

B) It generates context-aware suggestions by analyzing code patterns.

C) It stores user data for future use.

D) It replaces team collaboration tools.

Answer: B

Explanation: GitHub Copilot uses machine learning to analyze code patterns and provide context-aware suggestions. This makes it highly effective in assisting developers with both simple and complex tasks. It does not store user data or enforce coding standards.

70. Which of the following describes GitHub Copilot's integration with JetBrains IDEs?

A) Partial integration with limited functionality.

B) Full integration via a dedicated Copilot plugin.

C) Requires an external API for integration.

D) Only supports IntelliJ IDEA.

Answer: B

Explanation: GitHub Copilot offers full integration with JetBrains IDEs through a dedicated Copilot plugin. This ensures seamless functionality across supported JetBrains tools. It is not limited to IntelliJ IDEA but also supports PyCharm, WebStorm, and others.

71. What is the first step in enabling GitHub Copilot in Visual Studio Code?

A) Installing GitHub CLI

B) Installing the GitHub Copilot extension

C) Configuring a GitHub repository

D) Setting up a local server

Answer: B

Explanation: The first step in enabling GitHub Copilot in Visual Studio Code is installing the GitHub Copilot extension. Once installed, it integrates directly into the editor. No local server or CLI setup is required.

72. What happens if GitHub Copilot is unable to provide a suggestion?

A) It stops functioning until reinstalled.

B) It displays a message indicating no suggestions are available.

C) It automatically generates random code.

D) It requires a manual restart.

Answer: B

Explanation: If GitHub Copilot cannot provide a suggestion, it displays a message indicating that no suggestions are available. This typically happens when there is insufficient context for the AI to generate meaningful suggestions.

73. How can developers disable GitHub Copilot for specific file types in Visual Studio Code?

A) By modifying the Copilot settings in the VS Code extension menu.

B) By uninstalling the Copilot extension.

C) By creating a new GitHub account.

D) By disabling GitHub Actions.

Answer: A

Explanation: Developers can disable GitHub Copilot for specific file types by modifying its settings in the VS Code extension menu. This customization ensures that Copilot is only active where needed. It does not require uninstalling the extension.

74. What is the advantage of using GitHub Copilot for repetitive tasks?

A) It eliminates the need for debugging.

B) It automates repetitive tasks, saving development time.

C) It replaces the need for testing frameworks.

D) It generates project documentation.

Answer: B

Explanation: GitHub Copilot excels at automating repetitive tasks, allowing developers to focus on more complex and creative aspects of coding. This significantly reduces development time and enhances productivity. However, testing and debugging remain essential manual steps.

75. Which of the following is a key feature of GitHub Copilot for multi-language projects?

A) It requires switching languages manually.

B) It automatically adapts to the language being used in the editor.

C) It only supports one language per project.

D) It disables functionality for unsupported languages.

Answer: B

Explanation: GitHub Copilot automatically adapts to the language being used in the editor, providing relevant suggestions. This makes it highly effective for multi-language projects. No manual switching or reconfiguration is necessary.

76. How does GitHub Copilot enhance team collaboration?

A) By sharing project files automatically.

B) By providing consistent code suggestions across team members.

C) By managing GitHub repositories.

D) By automating project roadmaps.

Answer: B

Explanation: GitHub Copilot enhances collaboration by providing consistent and high-quality code suggestions across team members. This ensures uniformity in coding practices and reduces the time spent on repetitive tasks. It does not manage repositories or project roadmaps.

77. What is the role of context in GitHub Copilot's functionality?

A) It helps Copilot understand the surrounding code to provide accurate suggestions.

B) It stores user preferences for future use.

C) It enforces coding standards.

D) It replaces manual testing.

Answer: A

Explanation: Context helps GitHub Copilot analyze the surrounding code to generate accurate, relevant suggestions. This ensures that its output aligns with the specific requirements of the project. It does not store preferences or enforce standards.

78. Which of the following is required to use GitHub Copilot in a corporate environment?

A) GitHub Copilot Individual Plan

B) GitHub Copilot Enterprise Plan

C) A GitHub Free Account

D) GitHub CLI

Answer: B

Explanation: For corporate environments, the GitHub Copilot Enterprise Plan is required. It includes advanced features like Single Sign-On (SSO) and audit logs, ensuring compliance and security. Individual plans are not ideal for corporate use.

79. How does GitHub Copilot improve code quality?

A) By automatically fixing all errors.

B) By suggesting optimized and context-aware code snippets.

C) By enforcing strict coding guidelines.

D) By replacing manual code reviews.

Answer: B

Explanation: GitHub Copilot improves code quality by suggesting optimized and context-aware code snippets. While it does not replace manual reviews, it significantly reduces errors and improves efficiency. Developers must still validate the generated code.

80. What is the role of GitHub Copilot in educational projects?

A) It generates entire projects for students.

B) It provides real-time assistance and examples to help students learn coding.

C) It replaces coding instructors.

D) It automates grading for assignments.

Answer: B

Explanation: In educational projects, GitHub Copilot provides real-time assistance and examples, helping students learn coding more effectively. It acts as a supplementary tool for understanding programming concepts. It does not replace instructors or automate grading.

81. What is the default shortcut to cycle through GitHub Copilot suggestions?

A) Ctrl + N

B) Tab

C) Ctrl + Space

D) Shift + Alt + N

Answer: B

Explanation: Pressing Tab allows developers to cycle through GitHub Copilot's suggestions. This shortcut ensures quick and seamless navigation between suggested code snippets. It enhances workflow efficiency without disrupting the development process.

82. What type of feedback can developers provide to GitHub Copilot?

A) Feedback on code quality and relevance of suggestions.

B) Feedback on GitHub repository settings.

C) Feedback on deployment workflows.

D) Feedback on GitHub account billing.

Answer: A

Explanation: Developers can provide feedback on the quality and relevance of GitHub Copilot's suggestions. This helps improve the AI's performance over time. Repository settings, billing, and workflows are outside the scope of Copilot feedback.

83. Which of the following best defines GitHub Copilot?

A) A static code analysis tool

B) An AI-powered coding assistant integrated into IDEs

C) A repository management system

D) An automated deployment tool

Answer: B

Explanation: GitHub Copilot is an AI-powered coding assistant that integrates seamlessly into IDEs. It provides real-time code suggestions, enhances productivity, and supports multiple programming languages. It is not a static analysis or deployment tool.

Domain 2: Using GitHub Copilot for Coding

84. Which feature of GitHub Copilot is primarily used to generate code snippets?

A) GitHub Actions

B) AI-based context understanding

C) Static templates

D) Project management tools

Answer: B

Explanation: GitHub Copilot uses its AI-based context understanding to generate code snippets dynamically. It analyzes the surrounding code and comments to provide relevant suggestions. Unlike static templates, it adapts to the specific context of the developer's work.

85. How can you guide GitHub Copilot to generate specific code?

A) By writing clear comments describing the desired functionality.

B) By configuring the Copilot settings.

C) By enabling debugging mode.

D) By using a different IDE.

Answer: A

Explanation: Writing clear comments describing the desired functionality helps GitHub Copilot generate specific and accurate code suggestions. The AI interprets these comments as instructions. This is one of the most effective ways to guide Copilot.

86. What is the shortcut to accept a suggestion from GitHub Copilot in Visual Studio Code?

A) Ctrl + S

B) Tab

C) Shift + Enter

D) Alt + Space

Answer: B

Explanation: Pressing Tab in Visual Studio Code accepts a suggestion from GitHub Copilot. This shortcut ensures a seamless and efficient workflow. Developers can also cycle through suggestions using arrow keys before accepting one.

87. How does GitHub Copilot provide inline code suggestions?

A) By analyzing the entire project codebase.

B) By understanding the immediate context of the code being written.

C) By preloading all possible solutions.

D) By accessing external APIs.

Answer: B

Explanation: GitHub Copilot provides inline suggestions by understanding the immediate context of the code being written. It uses machine learning models to predict the next lines of code. This makes it highly efficient for real-time coding.

88. What is a limitation of GitHub Copilot when generating unit tests?

A) It cannot suggest any unit tests.

B) It only generates basic unit tests and may miss edge cases.

C) It requires a specific programming language.

D) It automatically runs the tests.

Answer: B

Explanation: GitHub Copilot is limited to generating basic unit tests and often misses edge cases or complex scenarios. Developers need to review and enhance the suggested tests for comprehensive coverage. It doesn't replace manual testing processes.

89. How does GitHub Copilot handle incomplete code snippets?

A) It ignores incomplete code.

B) It generates suggestions to complete the code.

C) It flags errors in the incomplete code.

D) It automatically deletes the incomplete code.

Answer: B

Explanation: GitHub Copilot generates suggestions to complete incomplete code snippets by analyzing the provided context. This helps developers write code faster and ensures continuity in the workflow. It doesn't flag errors or delete code.

90. What is a recommended practice for using GitHub Copilot when refactoring code?

A) Highlight the code and use context menu options like "Refactor with Copilot."

B) Automatically accept all suggestions.

C) Use Copilot for debugging only.

D) Disable Copilot during refactoring.

Answer: A

Explanation: To refactor code using GitHub Copilot, highlight the relevant section and use options like "Refactor with Copilot." This provides targeted suggestions for improving code quality. Developers should review the suggestions before applying them.

91. Which of the following best describes GitHub Copilot's inline suggestions?

A) Pre-written templates

B) AI-generated, context-aware code completions

C) Fixed code snippets

D) Documentation annotations

Answer: B

Explanation: GitHub Copilot's inline suggestions are AI-generated, context-aware code completions. They adapt to the specific programming context and user input. This makes them highly relevant and efficient for real-time coding.

92. What type of comments should developers use to guide GitHub Copilot effectively?

A) Vague comments describing high-level goals

B) Detailed comments explaining desired functionality and logic

C) Comments about unrelated topics

D) Comments in plain text files

Answer: B

Explanation: Detailed comments explaining the desired functionality and logic help GitHub Copilot generate accurate and relevant suggestions. The AI interprets these comments as specific instructions. Vague or irrelevant comments are less effective.

93. Which shortcut can you use to open GitHub Copilot's multi-line suggestions in Visual Studio Code?

A) Ctrl + Alt + Space

B) Ctrl + Enter

C) Shift + Tab

D) Alt + Enter

Answer: C

Explanation: Press Ctrl + Enter to open GitHub Copilot's multi-line suggestions in Visual Studio Code. This allows developers to preview and select the best suggestion for complex scenarios. It enhances productivity in multi-line coding tasks.

94. What is the most effective way to generate unit tests with GitHub Copilot?

A) Write a comment specifying the function to test and its expected behavior.

B) Run GitHub Copilot's auto-testing tool.

C) Use the "Generate Unit Tests" option in Copilot.

D) Highlight the code and press Shift + Enter.

Answer: A

Explanation: Writing a comment specifying the function to test and its expected behavior helps GitHub Copilot generate unit tests. This provides the AI with enough context to create relevant test cases. Developers should review and refine these tests for accuracy.

95. How does GitHub Copilot adapt to different programming languages?

A) It uses predefined syntax rules for all languages.

B) It automatically detects and adjusts suggestions based on the programming language being used.

C) It requires manual configuration for each language.

D) It only supports popular languages like Python and JavaScript.

Answer: B

Explanation: GitHub Copilot automatically detects the programming language being used and adjusts its suggestions accordingly. This ensures accurate and relevant code completions across various languages. It doesn't require manual configuration.

96. What is the primary role of GitHub Copilot when working with reusable code snippets?

A) Store snippets in a library.

B) Suggest optimized snippets based on context.

C) Flag outdated snippets.

D) Generate project documentation.

Answer: B

Explanation: GitHub Copilot suggests optimized reusable code snippets based on the context of the current task. This enhances efficiency by minimizing repetitive coding. It doesn't store or flag snippets but focuses on real-time assistance.

97. How can developers cycle through multiple suggestions from GitHub Copilot?

A) Use the Tab key.

B) Use the arrow keys.

C) Use Alt + Enter.

D) Use Ctrl + Space.

Answer: B

Explanation: Developers can cycle through multiple suggestions from GitHub Copilot using the arrow keys. This allows them to browse various options and select the most appropriate one. It's an essential feature for refining AI-generated code.

98. Which of the following is a limitation of GitHub Copilot in generating unit tests?

A) It can't generate tests for Python code.

B) It lacks understanding of complex business logic.

C) It disables manual testing workflows.

D) It ignores edge cases.

Answer: B

Explanation: GitHub Copilot may struggle to generate unit tests for complex business logic because such scenarios require deeper contextual understanding. Developers need to supplement Copilot's suggestions with manual input. It's best suited for straightforward test cases.

99. What is the role of GitHub Copilot in refactoring legacy code?

A) It automatically rewrites all legacy code.

B) It suggests improvements based on the existing code and comments.

C) It disables refactoring for unsupported languages.

D) It provides static templates for refactoring.

Answer: B

Explanation: GitHub Copilot suggests improvements for refactoring legacy code based on the existing code and comments. This helps streamline the process while retaining the original logic. Developers must review suggestions to ensure compatibility and correctness.

100. How does GitHub Copilot handle nested code structures?

A) It ignores them entirely.

B) It provides suggestions for both the outer and inner scopes.

C) It only suggests code for the outer scope.

D) It flags them as errors.

Answer: B

Explanation: GitHub Copilot analyzes both the outer and inner scopes of nested code structures to provide relevant suggestions. This ensures that the code is contextually accurate and fits seamlessly within the structure. Developers can refine suggestions as needed.

101. What happens if GitHub Copilot cannot generate code for a specific task?

A) It provides a generic message suggesting alternatives.

B) It stops functioning entirely.

C) It switches to a static template mode.

D) It requires reinstallation.

Answer: A

Explanation: If GitHub Copilot cannot generate code for a specific task, it provides a generic message suggesting alternatives. This typically occurs when the input lacks sufficient context. Developers can refine their comments or input to improve results.

102. How can GitHub Copilot assist in completing partially written functions?

A) By rewriting the entire function.

B) By providing suggestions to complete the function based on its context.

C) By disabling uncompleted functions.

D) By flagging incomplete code as errors.

Answer: B

Explanation: GitHub Copilot analyzes the context of a partially written function and provides suggestions to complete it. This speeds up the development process and ensures continuity. Developers should review the suggestions for accuracy.

103. Which of the following is NOT a recommended use case for

GitHub Copilot?

A) Learning a new programming language.

B) Writing boilerplate code.

C) Debugging complex legacy systems without context.

D) Generating basic unit tests.

Answer: C

Explanation: GitHub Copilot is not ideal for debugging complex legacy systems without sufficient context. While it excels at generating boilerplate code and basic tests, debugging often requires a deeper understanding that goes beyond Copilot's scope.

104. How does GitHub Copilot assist with writing repetitive boilerplate code?

A) It generates static templates for all projects.

B) It provides context-aware suggestions to automate repetitive sections.

C) It disables boilerplate code suggestions.

D) It requires manual input for repetitive code.

Answer: B

Explanation: GitHub Copilot assists developers by providing context-aware suggestions for automating repetitive boilerplate code. This reduces manual effort and saves time. It adapts to the specific structure of the project rather than using static templates.

105. What is the role of comments in guiding Copilot's suggestions for function generation?

A) Comments are ignored by Copilot.

B) Clear comments provide context, enabling Copilot to generate accurate functions.

C) Comments disable Copilot's functionality.

D) Comments are used purely for documentation.

Answer: B

Explanation: Clear comments provide context for GitHub Copilot, helping it generate accurate and relevant functions. Comments act as instructions for the AI, guiding it to create specific implementations. Poorly written or vague comments reduce suggestion quality.

106. What happens when you highlight a section of code and invoke Copilot's refactoring features?

A) The code is deleted.

B) Copilot suggests improvements or optimizations for the highlighted section.

C) The code is automatically rewritten.

D) Copilot disables refactoring for highlighted code.

Answer: B

Explanation: When you highlight a section of code and invoke Copilot's refactoring features, it suggests improvements or optimizations for that section. Developers can review and apply these suggestions selectively. The original code remains unchanged unless explicitly modified.

107. Which of the following is a limitation of Copilot's inline suggestions?

A) Works only for Python code.

B) Limited to the immediate context and may not understand larger project architecture.

C) Cannot handle simple tasks.

D) Only works with comments.

Answer: B

Explanation: Copilot's inline suggestions are limited to the immediate context and may not fully understand larger project architecture. This makes it ideal for short-term tasks but requires manual intervention for broader structural changes.

108. What is the recommended approach for reviewing Copilot-generated code?

A) Accept all suggestions without changes.

B) Review suggestions carefully for correctness and relevance.

C) Automatically apply suggestions in all cases.

D) Discard all suggestions.

Answer: B

Explanation: Developers should review Copilot-generated code carefully for correctness and relevance before applying it. This ensures the suggestions align with project requirements. Blindly accepting or discarding suggestions may lead to errors or inefficiencies.

109. How does Copilot handle incomplete variable declarations?

A) It ignores them.

B) It suggests completions based on the surrounding context.

C) It flags them as errors.

D) It disables further suggestions.

Answer: B

Explanation: Copilot analyzes the surrounding context and provides suggestions to complete incomplete variable declarations. This streamlines the development process and ensures continuity. Developers should validate these suggestions for accuracy.

110. How can you use Copilot to generate complex algorithms?

A) Write a detailed comment describing the algorithm.

B) Use the "Generate Algorithm" button.

C) Highlight existing code and press Tab.

D) Copilot cannot generate complex algorithms.

Answer: A

Explanation: To generate complex algorithms with Copilot, write a detailed comment describing the desired functionality. The AI interprets the comment and provides suggestions. This approach works best when the instructions are clear and specific.

111. Which shortcut allows you to view Copilot's alternative suggestions?

A) Ctrl + Tab

B) Alt + [Arrow Keys]

C) Ctrl + Enter

D) Shift + Space

Answer: B

Explanation: Pressing Alt + Arrow Keys allows you to view alternative suggestions from GitHub Copilot. This makes it easy to explore multiple solutions and choose the best one. It enhances flexibility in real-time coding scenarios.

112. What type of code can Copilot generate for unit tests?

A) Comprehensive tests covering all edge cases.

B) Basic unit tests based on function input and output.

C) Fully automated integration tests.

D) Tests for unsupported programming languages.

Answer: B

Explanation: Copilot can generate basic unit tests based on function input and output. However, it often misses edge cases and complex scenarios. Developers should enhance these tests manually to ensure full coverage.

113. What is the role of Copilot when generating SQL queries?

A) Automates database management.

B) Provides context-aware SQL query suggestions based on table names and schema.

C) Generates database schemas automatically.

D) Replaces SQL syntax entirely.

Answer: B

Explanation: Copilot provides context-aware SQL query suggestions based on the table names, schema, and comments provided in the code. This accelerates query creation while maintaining accuracy. It does not replace database management tasks.

114. What happens if Copilot generates code that includes sensitive information, such as API keys?

A) Copilot automatically flags and removes sensitive information.

B) Developers are responsible for reviewing and removing such information.

C) Copilot encrypts the information.

D) Copilot disables the suggestion.

Answer: B

Explanation: Developers are responsible for reviewing and removing sensitive information, such as API keys, from Copilot's generated code. While Copilot avoids generating sensitive data intentionally, oversight is essential to ensure security.

115. How does Copilot handle function overloading in languages like C++?

A) It disables suggestions for overloaded functions.

B) It provides suggestions for each overloaded function based on the context.

C) It combines all overloaded functions into a single suggestion.

D) It ignores overloaded functions.

Answer: B

Explanation: Copilot provides suggestions for each overloaded function based on the specific context in C++ or similar languages. This ensures that the correct version of the function is implemented. Developers can refine the suggestions as needed.

116. What's a best practice for guiding Copilot in generating REST API endpoints?

A) Write a comment with the HTTP method and endpoint details.

B) Use Copilot's "API Generator" tool.

C) Highlight existing endpoints and press Tab.

D) Copilot cannot generate REST API endpoints.

Answer: A

Explanation: Writing a comment with the HTTP method (e.g., GET, POST) and endpoint details helps Copilot generate relevant REST API endpoints. This ensures that the generated code aligns with the application's requirements.

117. What is the expected output when Copilot generates code for mathematical functions?

A) Perfectly optimized mathematical solutions.

B) Approximate solutions that may require manual adjustments.

C) A syntax error.

D) A list of mathematical theories.

Answer: B

Explanation: Copilot generates approximate solutions for mathematical functions based on the provided context. These solutions may require manual adjustments for optimization or accuracy. It does not guarantee error-free outputs.

118. How does Copilot handle nested loops in complex scenarios?

A) It suggests optimized loop structures based on the context.

B) It disables suggestions for nested loops.

C) It automatically rewrites the entire loop.

D) It ignores nested structures.

Answer: A

Explanation: Copilot suggests optimized loop structures for nested scenarios, ensuring efficiency and readability. Developers can refine these suggestions to suit specific requirements. It does not rewrite or disable nested loops automatically.

119. How does Copilot assist in debugging incomplete code blocks?

A) By automatically fixing the code.

B) By suggesting completions and highlighting potential issues.

C) By disabling suggestions for incomplete blocks.

D) By running automated tests.

Answer: B

Explanation: Copilot suggests completions for incomplete code blocks and highlights potential issues based on context. This helps developers debug and complete their code efficiently. It does not run automated tests but assists in resolving errors.

120. What is a key limitation of using Copilot for advanced data structures?

A) It only supports basic data structures.

B) It may not fully understand custom or highly complex data structures.

C) It disables suggestions for advanced algorithms.

D) It cannot generate code for arrays.

Answer: B

Explanation: Copilot may struggle with custom or highly complex data structures, as these often require in-depth understanding beyond its training. It works best with standard or well-documented structures.

121. How does Copilot assist in generating file-handling functions?

A) By providing templates for standard file operations.

B) By writing file-handling code based on comments and context.

C) By disabling file-related tasks.

D) By automatically opening files in the IDE.

Answer: B

Explanation: Copilot generates file-handling code (e.g., reading, writing) based on comments and surrounding context. This speeds up the implementation of common file operations while ensuring accuracy. Developers should validate the generated code.

122. What is Copilot's role in writing recursive functions?

A) It avoids recursive function suggestions.

B) It assists in writing and optimizing recursive functions based on context.

C) It disables recursion for optimization.

D) It generates infinite loops.

Answer: B

Explanation: Copilot assists in writing recursive functions by analyzing the context and providing relevant suggestions. It ensures that the recursion structure is logical and efficient. Developers must validate to avoid infinite loops or errors.

123. How does Copilot handle code comments during generation?

A) It replaces all existing comments with new ones.

B) It uses comments to guide code generation while preserving them.

C) It ignores comments entirely.

D) It disables suggestions for commented sections.

Answer: B

Explanation: Copilot uses comments to guide code generation while preserving them for future reference. This ensures that the code aligns with the developer's intent. Comments remain intact unless explicitly modified.

124. How does GitHub Copilot assist in generating loops for data processing?

A) It generates loops automatically based on variable names.

B) It provides context-aware suggestions for loop structures.

C) It disables loop generation for unsupported data types.

D) It replaces all existing loops with new ones.

Answer: B

Explanation: GitHub Copilot provides context-aware suggestions for loop structures based on the surrounding code and comments. This ensures the generated loop aligns with the intended functionality.

Developers should review these suggestions for correctness.

125. What should developers do to ensure Copilot generates efficient code?

A) Use broad, generic comments.

B) Provide specific and detailed comments to guide the AI.

C) Leave the code context empty.

D) Use Copilot without any input.

Answer: B

Explanation: Providing specific and detailed comments helps GitHub Copilot generate efficient and relevant code. Clear guidance ensures the AI understands the developer's intent. This leads to better quality suggestions.

126. How does Copilot handle suggestions for functions with multiple parameters?

A) It generates suggestions for all parameters based on context.

B) It disables suggestions for multi-parameter functions.

C) It requires manual input for all parameters.

D) It only suggests the first parameter.

Answer: A

Explanation: Copilot generates suggestions for all parameters of a function based on the context, including their types and use cases. This streamlines coding for multi-parameter functions. Developers should validate the generated parameters.

127. What is the key benefit of using Copilot for refactoring code?

A) It eliminates the need for manual reviews.

B) It provides optimized suggestions for improving readability and efficiency.

C) It disables debugging for refactored code.

D) It rewrites the entire codebase automatically.

Answer: B

Explanation: Copilot provides optimized suggestions for refactoring code, improving both readability and efficiency. This reduces time spent on manual adjustments. Developers should review and apply these suggestions selectively.

128. How does Copilot assist with switch-case structures in programming?

A) It generates switch-case structures based on the surrounding code and comments.

B) It disables suggestions for switch-case statements.

C) It only supports if-else structures.

D) It automatically converts switch-case to if-else.

Answer: A

Explanation: Copilot generates switch-case structures based on the context provided in the surrounding code and comments. This accelerates coding for decision-making scenarios. Developers should verify the generated cases.

129. Which of the following is a best practice for testing Copilot-

generated unit tests?

A) Rely entirely on Copilot-generated tests without review.

B) Manually review and enhance the generated tests for edge cases.

C) Disable other testing tools when using Copilot.

D) Only use Copilot for integration tests.

Answer: B

Explanation: Manually reviewing and enhancing Copilot-generated tests ensures they cover all edge cases and meet project requirements. Copilot is not a replacement for thorough testing. It complements manual testing processes.

130. What is the role of Copilot in generating error-handling code?

A) It disables suggestions for error handling.

B) It suggests error-handling logic based on the context.

C) It automatically fixes all errors in the code.

D) It flags errors without providing solutions.

Answer: B

Explanation: Copilot suggests error-handling logic based on the context, helping developers implement robust error management. These suggestions can include try-catch blocks or conditional checks. Developers must validate the generated code for reliability.

131. How does Copilot assist in creating recursive algorithms?

A) It suggests base cases and recursive steps based on comments and context.

B) It disables recursion for unsupported languages.

C) It automatically generates iterative solutions instead.

D) It rewrites existing algorithms without validation.

Answer: A

Explanation: Copilot assists in creating recursive algorithms by suggesting base cases and recursive steps based on the provided context. This simplifies the development of complex algorithms. Validation is essential to avoid infinite loops or errors.

132. What should developers do if Copilot generates suboptimal code for a specific task?

A) Accept the code and use it as-is.

B) Refine the comments or context to improve the suggestions.

C) Disable Copilot for that task.

D) Reinstall the Copilot extension.

Answer: B

Explanation: If Copilot generates suboptimal code, developers should refine the comments or context to improve the suggestions. This provides the AI with better guidance for generating relevant and optimized code.

133. How does Copilot handle context when generating code for nested functions?

A) It ignores nested functions entirely.

B) It provides context-aware suggestions for both parent and nested functions.

C) It disables suggestions for nested structures.

D) It combines all nested functions into a single block.

Answer: B

Explanation: Copilot provides context-aware suggestions for both parent and nested functions, ensuring the generated code fits seamlessly within the structure. This is particularly useful for complex, multi-layered functions.

134. What is a major limitation of Copilot when generating solutions for complex algorithms?

A) It cannot generate any algorithms.

B) It may generate solutions that lack optimization or miss edge cases.

C) It disables suggestions for advanced algorithms.

D) It requires manual algorithm coding.

Answer: B

Explanation: Copilot may generate solutions for complex algorithms that lack optimization or miss edge cases. Developers should review and refine these suggestions to ensure they meet performance and functional requirements.

135. Which programming construct is NOT directly supported by Copilot for code suggestions?

A) Loops (for, while)

B) Conditional statements (if, else)

C) Database schemas

D) Variable declarations

Answer: C

Explanation: Copilot does not directly support generating database schemas but can assist with SQL queries related to the schema. It excels at providing suggestions for loops, conditionals, and variable declarations.

136. How does Copilot assist in writing modular code?

A) By enforcing modular design principles.

B) By providing suggestions to encapsulate functionality into reusable functions.

C) By disabling suggestions for non-modular code.

D) By automatically rewriting all code into modules.

Answer: B

Explanation: Copilot provides suggestions to encapsulate functionality into reusable functions, promoting modularity in code. This improves readability, maintainability, and scalability. Developers retain full control over the modularization process.

137. What is the role of Copilot in generating class-based code structures?

A) It only supports procedural code.

B) It suggests class definitions and methods based on the context.

C) It disables suggestions for object-oriented approaches.

D) It automatically refactors procedural code into classes.

Answer: B

Explanation: Copilot suggests class definitions and methods based on the surrounding context and comments. This accelerates the development of object-oriented code structures. Developers should review and refine the suggestions for alignment with project requirements.

138. How does Copilot handle incomplete comments?

A) It ignores them entirely.

B) It attempts to infer the developer's intent and generate relevant code.

C) It flags them as errors.

D) It disables suggestions for incomplete comments.

Answer: B

Explanation: Copilot attempts to infer the developer's intent from incomplete comments and generates relevant code accordingly. However, providing detailed and complete comments ensures better suggestions.

139. What is the expected behavior when Copilot generates code for sorting algorithms?

A) It generates optimized solutions for common sorting methods (e.g., quicksort, mergesort).

B) It disables sorting suggestions for complex data structures.

C) It only supports bubble sort.

D) It rewrites all existing sorting code.

Answer: A

Explanation: Copilot generates optimized solutions for common sorting methods like quicksort, mergesort, and others, based on the context provided. Developers should review the suggested code for correctness and efficiency.

140. How does Copilot assist in integrating external APIs?

A) It generates API integration code based on comments and context.

B) It disables suggestions for external APIs.

C) It only supports built-in APIs.

D) It automatically tests all integrated APIs.

Answer: A

Explanation: Copilot generates API integration code using comments and surrounding context, helping developers quickly set up external API calls. Validation and testing remain the developer's responsibility.

141. What is Copilot's role in writing code for event-driven programming?

A) It suggests event handlers and triggers based on the context.

B) It disables event-driven programming support.

C) It replaces event listeners with static code.

D) It flags all events as errors.

Answer: A

Explanation: Copilot assists in event-driven programming by suggesting event handlers and triggers based on the provided code and comments. This accelerates the implementation of event-based workflows.

142. How can developers improve Copilot's suggestions for complex data transformations?

A) Provide detailed comments outlining the transformation logic.

B) Use generic placeholders for data.

C) Disable Copilot and code manually.

D) Avoid using Copilot for transformations.

Answer: A

Explanation: Providing detailed comments outlining the transformation logic helps Copilot generate accurate suggestions for complex data transformations. This ensures the output aligns with the developer's intent.

143. How does Copilot handle suggestions for asynchronous programming?

A) It suggests async functions and awaits based on the context.

B) It disables asynchronous code suggestions.

C) It automatically converts all code to synchronous.

D) It flags all async code as errors.

Answer: A

Explanation: Copilot suggests async functions and awaits based on the context provided, helping developers implement asynchronous workflows efficiently. Developers should validate the suggestions for correctness.

Domain 3: GitHub Copilot Chat

144. What is the primary purpose of GitHub Copilot Chat?

A) Automating deployments

B) Answering questions about the codebase and generating explanations

C) Managing repositories

D) Replacing manual debugging

Answer: B

Explanation: GitHub Copilot Chat is designed to answer questions about the codebase and provide explanations for existing code. It enhances understanding and debugging efficiency. It complements developers' efforts rather than replacing manual tasks.

145. Which feature of GitHub Copilot Chat helps in learning new programming languages?

A) Auto-deployment

B) Real-time syntax suggestions and code explanations

C) Code refactoring tools

D) Repository management

Answer: B

Explanation: GitHub Copilot Chat assists in learning new programming languages by providing real-time syntax suggestions and detailed explanations of code. It allows developers to ask questions and receive practical examples. This accelerates the learning process.

146. How can a developer invoke GitHub Copilot Chat in supported IDEs?

A) By enabling GitHub Actions

B) By typing a question in the chat window

C) By running a command in the terminal

D) By creating a pull request

Answer: B

Explanation: Developers can invoke GitHub Copilot Chat by typing a question directly into the chat window of supported IDEs. The AI provides responses based on the context of the code. This makes it a seamless addition to the coding workflow.

147. What type of questions can developers ask GitHub Copilot Chat?

A) Only syntax-related questions

B) Questions about the codebase, debugging, and explanations of logic

C) Deployment-related questions

D) Repository management queries

Answer: B

Explanation: Developers can ask GitHub Copilot Chat questions about the codebase, debugging, and logic explanations. It is designed to assist with understanding and improving code. Deployment and repository management are outside its scope.

148. Which command allows developers to ask GitHub Copilot Chat for an explanation of a specific function?

A) Highlight the function and type a question in the chat.

B) Call the GitHub CLI.

C) Run explain() in the terminal.

D) Enable GitHub Actions.

Answer: A

Explanation: Developers can highlight the function and type a question in GitHub Copilot Chat to get an explanation. The AI analyzes the context and provides a detailed response. This makes it easy to understand complex functions.

149. What is a key limitation of GitHub Copilot Chat when answering questions about code?

A) It cannot analyze external libraries.

B) It may provide incomplete or context-dependent answers.

C) It only works with Python.

D) It requires manual input for all responses.

Answer: B

Explanation: GitHub Copilot Chat may provide incomplete or context-dependent answers, especially if it lacks sufficient context from the codebase. Developers must verify the information provided. It supports multiple programming languages.

150. How does GitHub Copilot Chat assist in debugging?

A) By automatically fixing all errors.

B) By analyzing the code and suggesting potential fixes.

C) By disabling error-prone sections of code.

D) By running automated tests.

Answer: B

Explanation: GitHub Copilot Chat assists in debugging by analyzing code and suggesting potential fixes based on the context. It helps identify issues and provides targeted solutions. Developers retain full control over implementing the suggestions.

151. Can GitHub Copilot Chat answer high-level questions about project architecture?

A) Yes, if sufficient context is provided in the codebase.

B) No, it only works for line-by-line code.

C) Yes, but only for Python projects.

D) No, it cannot analyze architecture.

Answer: A

Explanation: GitHub Copilot Chat can answer high-level questions about project architecture if sufficient context is available in the codebase. It provides insights based on its understanding of the overall structure.

152. What is the role of Copilot Chat in explaining error messages?

A) It disables error-related queries.

B) It provides explanations and potential solutions for error messages.

C) It generates random solutions.

D) It replaces the need for error logs.

Answer: B

Explanation: Copilot Chat analyzes error messages and provides explanations along with potential solutions. This helps developers resolve issues quickly. It does not replace error logs but enhances their usability.

153. How can developers use GitHub Copilot Chat for learning best practices in coding?

A) By asking for refactoring suggestions.

B) By enabling GitHub Actions.

C) By running automated workflows.

D) By disabling the chat feature.

Answer: A

Explanation: Developers can use GitHub Copilot Chat to learn best practices by asking for refactoring suggestions and explanations of code. It offers insights into improving code quality and adhering to standards.

154. What happens if Copilot Chat doesn't have enough context to answer a question?

A) It provides a generic response or asks for more information.

B) It disables the chat feature.

C) It generates random answers.

D) It stops functioning.

Answer: A

Explanation: If Copilot Chat lacks sufficient context, it provides a generic response or asks the developer for more information. This ensures the AI remains helpful within its limitations.

155. How does Copilot Chat assist in learning new frameworks?

A) By providing tutorials.

B) By generating code snippets and explaining framework-specific logic.

C) By replacing the need for documentation.

D) By automating framework installation.

Answer: B

Explanation: Copilot Chat assists in learning new frameworks by generating code snippets and explaining framework-specific logic. This complements official documentation and accelerates the learning process.

156. How can Copilot Chat help developers understand legacy code?

A) By rewriting the entire codebase.

B) By providing explanations for specific code sections.

C) By replacing legacy functions with new ones.

D) By disabling suggestions for old code.

Answer: B

Explanation: Copilot Chat helps developers understand legacy code by providing explanations for specific functions or code sections. This makes it easier to analyze and maintain older codebases.

157. What is the best way to use Copilot Chat for debugging a specific error?

A) Highlight the error message and ask for a solution in the chat.

B) Run automated workflows.

C) Disable the error-prone code.

D) Copy the code into a separate file.

Answer: A

Explanation: Highlighting the error message and asking for a solution in Copilot Chat allows the AI to analyze and suggest targeted fixes. This streamlines the debugging process.

158. Can Copilot Chat generate explanations for external libraries or APIs?

A) Yes, if the libraries are well-documented and referenced in the code.

B) No, it only works for built-in functions.

C) Yes, but only for Python APIs.

D) No, it cannot analyze external resources.

Answer: A

Explanation: Copilot Chat can generate explanations for external libraries or APIs if they are well-documented and referenced in the code. This helps developers integrate and use external tools effectively.

159. What is a limitation of using Copilot Chat for code explanations?

A) It cannot provide explanations for complex logic.

B) It may provide incomplete answers without sufficient context.

C) It only works for open-source projects.

D) It disables manual explanations.

Answer: B

Explanation: Copilot Chat may provide incomplete answers if it lacks sufficient context from the codebase. Developers should supplement these answers with additional research when needed.

160. How does Copilot Chat assist in learning new programming paradigms?

A) By running tutorials.

B) By explaining code snippets and comparing paradigms.

C) By automating project set-up.

D) By generating project documentation.

Answer: B

Explanation: Copilot Chat assists in learning new programming paradigms by explaining code snippets and comparing paradigms like procedural, functional, and object-oriented programming. This enhances developers' understanding.

161. Can GitHub Copilot Chat assist with optimizing code performance?

A) Yes, by suggesting performance improvements based on context.

B) No, it only works for debugging.

C) Yes, but only for Python code.

D) No, it cannot analyze performance.

Answer: A

Explanation: GitHub Copilot Chat can suggest performance improvements based on context, helping developers optimize their code. These suggestions should be validated against real-world requirements.

162. How can Copilot Chat be used for collaborative coding?

A) By sharing code snippets and explanations within a team.

B) By automating pull request reviews.

C) By replacing manual collaboration tools.

D) By generating team communication logs.

Answer: A

Explanation: Copilot Chat can be used for collaborative coding by sharing code snippets, explanations, and suggestions within a team. This fosters better communication and understanding among team members.

163. What is a key benefit of using GitHub Copilot Business for multinational teams?

A) Automatic code refactoring

B) Support for compliance with global data privacy regulations like GDPR

C) Unlimited repository creation

D) Faster pull request approvals

Answer: B

Explanation: GitHub Copilot Business supports compliance with global data privacy regulations like GDPR, ensuring that multinational teams can work securely across different jurisdictions.

164. How does GitHub Copilot Enterprise enhance security during user authentication?

A) By using multi-factor authentication (MFA) with Single Sign-On (SSO)

B) By disabling all manual logins

C) By encrypting user passwords locally

D) By allowing anonymous access to repositories

Answer: A

Explanation: GitHub Copilot Enterprise enhances security during user authentication by integrating multi-factor authentication (MFA) with Single Sign-On (SSO), reducing the risk of unauthorized access.

165. What feature of GitHub Copilot Business allows teams to prevent unauthorized code changes?

A) Centralized role-based access controls

B) Automated testing workflows

C) Repository duplication tools

D) Automatic code merging

Answer: A

Explanation: Centralized role-based access controls allow teams to prevent unauthorized code changes by restricting access to specific users or roles.

166. Which feature of GitHub Copilot Business ensures visibility into how team members are using the tool?

A) Automated code suggestions

B) Audit logs for tracking team activity

C) Unlimited public repositories

D) Auto-generated documentation

Answer: B

Explanation: Audit logs ensure visibility into how team members are using GitHub Copilot, enabling administrators to monitor activity and maintain compliance.

167. How does GitHub Copilot Business help teams manage seat allocations?

A) By automatically assigning licenses

B) By offering centralized billing and seat management

C) By disabling unused seats

D) By generating automated reports for individual users

Answer: B

Explanation: GitHub Copilot Business helps teams manage seat allocations by providing centralized billing and seat management, simplifying resource allocation and license tracking.

168. What is a key benefit of using GitHub Copilot in a self-hosted environment?

A) Reduced latency in code suggestions

B) Enhanced control over infrastructure and compliance

C) Automatic pull request generation

D) Unlimited private repositories

Answer: B

Explanation: Using GitHub Copilot in a self-hosted environment provides enhanced control over infrastructure and compliance, making it suitable for organizations with specific security requirements.

169. Which compliance-related feature is supported by GitHub Copilot Business?

A) Automated deployment pipelines

B) Adherence to standards like GDPR, HIPAA, and ISO 27001

C) Unlimited seat licenses

D) Auto-generated pull requests

Answer: B

Explanation: GitHub Copilot Business supports compliance with standards like GDPR, HIPAA, and ISO 27001, ensuring organizations meet regulatory requirements.

170. How does centralized management in GitHub Copilot Business benefit administrators?

A) By automating code reviews

B) By allowing them to manage access, seats, and billing from a single dashboard

C) By generating random security reports

D) By disabling manual coding workflows

Answer: B

Explanation: Centralized management allows administrators to manage access, seats, and billing from a single dashboard, providing easy control over organizational resources.

171. What is the role of GitHub Copilot Business in regulatory compliance?

A) It automatically generates compliance reports.

B) It ensures adherence to data privacy laws like GDPR through audit logs and encryption.

C) It disables non-compliant repositories.

D) It replaces manual coding workflows.

Answer: B

Explanation: GitHub Copilot Business ensures adherence to data privacy laws like GDPR through features like audit logs, encryption, and secure access controls.

172. Which feature of GitHub Copilot Business simplifies license management for teams?

A) Unlimited free users

B) Centralized billing and license tracking

C) Automated user seat allocation

D) Disabling unused licenses

Answer: B

Explanation: Centralized billing and license tracking simplify team license management, ensuring that resources are allocated efficiently and costs are managed effectively.

173. What is a key feature of GitHub Copilot Business that supports team scalability?

A) Automated testing tools

B) Role-based access controls and centralized management

C) Auto-generated repository backups

D) Unlimited public repositories

Answer: B

Explanation: Role-based access controls and centralized management support team scalability by streamlining access management and ensuring secure collaboration as teams grow.

174. How does GitHub Copilot Enterprise address concerns about sensitive data?

A) By offering encrypted communication and adherence to privacy standards

B) By disabling sensitive repositories

C) By storing all data locally on user machines

D) By deleting audit logs every 30 days

Answer: A

Explanation: GitHub Copilot Enterprise addresses concerns about sensitive data through encrypted communication and adherence to privacy standards like GDPR and HIPAA.

175. What is the primary function of audit logs in GitHub Copilot Business?

A) To automate repository creation

B) To track team activities and ensure compliance

C) To generate random security reports

D) To disable manual coding workflows

Answer: B

Explanation: Audit logs track team activities and ensure compliance, helping organizations maintain visibility and accountability in their workflows.

176. What is a key advantage of using GitHub Copilot Business in cloud-hosted environments?

A) Unlimited repository backups

B) Scalability and reduced dependency on local infrastructure

C) Automatic repository duplication

D) Auto-generated pull requests

Answer: B

Explanation: Using GitHub Copilot Business in cloud-hosted environments provides scalability and reduces dependency on local infrastructure, enabling seamless team collaboration.

177. Which feature in GitHub Copilot Business ensures secure team collaboration?

A) Auto-generated unit tests

B) Role-based access controls and SSO integration

C) Unlimited free seats

D) Automated testing tools

Answer: B

Explanation: Role-based access controls and SSO integration ensure secure team collaboration by restricting access to authorized users only.

178. How does GitHub Copilot Business handle compliance in regulated industries?

A) By generating compliance certificates automatically

B) By adhering to standards like GDPR, HIPAA, and ISO 27001

C) By disabling manual coding workflows

D) By allowing anonymous repository access

Answer: B

Explanation: GitHub Copilot Business handles compliance in regulated industries by adhering to standards like GDPR, HIPAA, and ISO 27001, ensuring organizations meet legal requirements.

179. What is the role of centralized billing in GitHub Copilot Business?

A) To allocate resources automatically

B) To consolidate team costs into a single invoice

C) To disable unused licenses

D) To generate random financial reports

Answer: B

Explanation: Centralized billing consolidates team costs into a single invoice, simplifying financial management for organizations with multiple users.

180. How does GitHub Copilot Business improve security for enterprise teams?

A) By offering audit logs and encryption for sensitive data

B) By disabling unused repositories automatically

C) By replacing manual coding workflows

D) By generating random security alerts

Answer: A

Explanation: GitHub Copilot Business improves security by offering audit logs and encryption for sensitive data, ensuring secure collaboration for enterprise teams.

181. What is a key compliance feature in GitHub Copilot Business?

A) Unlimited code generation

B) Adherence to privacy regulations and secure access controls

C) Automated repository creation

D) Role-based licensing

Answer: B

Explanation: Adherence to privacy regulations like GDPR and secure access controls ensures compliance, making GitHub Copilot Business suitable for regulated industries.

182. How does GitHub Copilot Business support administrators in managing large teams?

A) By automating seat allocation

B) By providing centralized tools for billing, access, and activity tracking

C) By disabling unused repositories

D) By generating automated compliance reports

Answer: B

Explanation: GitHub Copilot Business provides administrators with centralized tools for billing, access management, and activity tracking, simplifying the management of large teams.

Domain 4: Advanced Features for Teams and Enterprises

183. Which GitHub Copilot plan is best suited for enterprise teams?

A) Copilot Individual

B) Copilot Business

C) Copilot Open Source

D) Copilot Community

Answer: B

Explanation: GitHub Copilot Business is designed for enterprise teams, offering features like centralized management, Single Sign-On (SSO), and compliance tools to meet organizational needs.

184. What is the primary purpose of Single Sign-On (SSO) in GitHub Copilot Business?

A) To centralize user authentication for enhanced security.

B) To enable multiple users to share one login.

C) To automate pull request approvals.

D) To disable manual authentication.

Answer: A

Explanation: SSO centralizes user authentication, integrating with identity providers like Okta or Azure AD, ensuring secure and streamlined access for organizational users.

185. Which feature in GitHub Copilot Business allows organizations to track team activity?

A) Role-based access controls

B) Centralized billing

C) Audit logs

D) Automated deployments

Answer: C

Explanation: Audit logs provide visibility into team activity, enabling organizations to monitor usage, ensure compliance, and detect unauthorized actions.

186. How does centralized management benefit administrators in GitHub Copilot Business?

A) It automates code reviews.

B) It allows administrators to manage user access and seat allocation.

C) It disables unused repositories.

D) It generates automated compliance reports.

Answer: B

Explanation: Centralized management enables administrators to control user access, allocate seats, and oversee billing, simplifying resource management across teams.

187. What is a key compliance feature of GitHub Copilot Business?

A) Automated testing tools

B) Adherence to data protection standards like GDPR

C) Unlimited public repository access

D) Auto-generated code refactoring

Answer: B

Explanation: GitHub Copilot Business ensures compliance with data protection standards like GDPR, making it suitable for organizations with strict regulatory requirements.

188. Which hosting environments are supported by GitHub Copilot for Enterprises?

A) Only cloud-hosted environments

B) Only self-hosted environments

C) Both cloud-hosted and self-hosted environments

D) Only on-premise servers

Answer: C

Explanation: GitHub Copilot for Enterprises supports both cloud-hosted and self-hosted environments, providing flexibility for organizations with diverse infrastructure needs.

189. What is the primary benefit of audit logs in GitHub Copilot Business?

A) They automate code generation.

B) They enhance security by providing visibility into user activities.

C) They disable unauthorized repositories.

D) They automatically approve pull requests.

Answer: B

Explanation: Audit logs improve security by tracking user activities, ensuring compliance, and providing transparency into organizational workflows.

190. What is a key advantage of using self-hosted environments with GitHub Copilot?

A) Reduced dependency on cloud infrastructure.

B) Automatic pull request merging.

C) Unlimited free seats for teams.

D) Faster code generation speeds.

Answer: A

Explanation: Self-hosted environments provide enhanced control over data security and reduce dependency on external cloud infrastructure, making them ideal for organizations with specific compliance needs.

191. Which feature of GitHub Copilot Business simplifies financial management for teams?

A) Centralized billing for all team members

B) Automated pull request approvals

C) Unlimited repository creation

D) Role-based access controls

Answer: A

Explanation: Centralized billing consolidates costs for the entire team into a single invoice, streamlining financial management for organizations.

192. Which compliance standards does GitHub Copilot Business support?

A) Agile Development Framework

B) GDPR, HIPAA, and ISO 27001

C) Repository mirroring

D) DevOps pipelines

Answer: B

Explanation: GitHub Copilot Business adheres to compliance standards like GDPR, HIPAA, and ISO 27001, addressing the needs of regulated industries.

193. How does GitHub Copilot Business ensure data privacy for organizations?

A) By encrypting all communications and adhering to privacy regulations.

B) By storing data locally on user devices.

C) By disabling private repositories.

D) By generating random passwords for repositories.

Answer: A

Explanation: GitHub Copilot Business ensures data privacy by encrypting communications and adhering to regulations like GDPR, protecting sensitive organizational data.

194. What is the role of role-based access controls in GitHub Copilot Business?

A) To automate repository creation.

B) To restrict access to resources based on user roles.

C) To generate code snippets automatically.

D) To disable unused repositories.

Answer: B

Explanation: Role-based access controls restrict access to resources based on user roles, enhancing security by ensuring users have access only to what they need.

195. Why is centralized management important for large teams using GitHub Copilot Business?

A) To automate all pull requests.

B) To provide a single dashboard for managing users, seats, and billing.

C) To disable manual coding tasks.

D) To increase repository visibility.

Answer: B

Explanation: Centralized management provides a single dashboard for managing users, seats, and billing, simplifying resource allocation and oversight for large teams.

196. How does GitHub Copilot Business support compliance audits?

A) By generating compliance certificates automatically.

B) By providing detailed audit logs of user activities.

C) By disabling repositories during audits.

D) By replacing manual audits with AI-driven processes.

Answer: B

Explanation: Audit logs in GitHub Copilot Business provide detailed records of user activities, making compliance audits easier and more transparent.

197. What is a limitation of GitHub Copilot in self-hosted environments?

A) Reduced support for private repositories.

B) Limited access to certain cloud-based features.

C) Lack of compliance tracking tools.

D) Disabling of code generation features.

Answer: B

Explanation: Self-hosted environments may have limited access to some cloud-based features, but they offer enhanced control over data security and compliance.

198. Which feature of GitHub Copilot Business enhances security for enterprise teams?

A) Automated pull request approvals

B) Integration with Single Sign-On (SSO)

C) Unlimited public repositories

D) Automated testing tools

Answer: B

Explanation: Integration with Single Sign-On (SSO) enhances security by centralizing authentication and reducing the risk of unauthorized access.

199. How does GitHub Copilot Business handle sensitive data in private repositories?

A) By encrypting all data and adhering to compliance standards.

B) By disabling access to private repositories.

C) By storing sensitive data locally.

D) By automatically deleting audit logs.

Answer: A

Explanation: GitHub Copilot Business encrypts all data and adheres to compliance standards, ensuring the security of sensitive information in private repositories.

200. What is the primary benefit of using GitHub Copilot Business in cloud-hosted environments?

A) Reduced dependency on local infrastructure.

B) Automated repository creation.

C) Enhanced manual coding workflows.

D) Unlimited private repository access.

Answer: A

Explanation: Using GitHub Copilot Business in cloud-hosted environments reduces dependency on local infrastructure, enabling seamless collaboration from anywhere.

201. Which feature of GitHub Copilot Business ensures secure collaboration across teams?

A) Automated testing tools

B) Role-based access controls and centralized management

C) Unlimited pull request approvals

D) Repository duplication tools

Answer: B

Explanation: Role-based access controls and centralized management enable secure collaboration by restricting access and providing administrators with oversight.

202. Why is compliance important for organizations using GitHub Copilot Business?

A) To automate testing processes.

B) To meet legal and regulatory requirements for data protection.

C) To enable faster pull request approvals.

D) To simplify repository management.

Answer: B

Explanation: Compliance ensures organizations meet legal and regulatory requirements for data protection, making GitHub Copilot Business suitable for regulated industries.

203. What is the main role of Single Sign-On (SSO) in GitHub Copilot Business?

A) To allow anonymous access to repositories.

B) To centralize authentication for all team members using an identity provider.

C) To create automated pull requests.

D) To enable unlimited free seats for the team.

Answer: B

Explanation: SSO centralizes authentication for all team members, integrating with identity providers like Okta, Azure AD, or Google Workspace, enhancing security and simplifying access management.

204. Which compliance feature of GitHub Copilot Business ensures adherence to HIPAA?

A) Role-based access controls

B) Adherence to strict data encryption and privacy standards

C) Unlimited repository creation

D) Automated pull request approvals

Answer: B

Explanation: GitHub Copilot Business adheres to strict data encryption and privacy standards, ensuring compliance with regulations like HIPAA for organizations in sensitive industries.

205. What is the benefit of using GitHub Copilot Business in a hybrid environment?

A) Automated repository creation.

B) Flexibility to use both cloud-hosted and self-hosted setups.

C) Faster code generation in cloud environments.

D) Unlimited public repositories.

Answer: B

Explanation: A hybrid environment allows organizations to use both cloud-hosted and self-hosted setups, providing flexibility to meet specific compliance and infrastructure needs.

206. What is the purpose of audit logs in GitHub Copilot Business?

A) To automate testing workflows.

B) To track user activity and ensure compliance with organizational policies.

C) To disable unused repositories.

D) To generate code snippets automatically.

Answer: B

Explanation: Audit logs track user activity and ensure compliance with organizational policies, offering transparency and accountability for team actions.

207. Which feature of GitHub Copilot Business enhances collaboration security?

A) Automated pull request generation.

B) Role-based access controls and centralized management.

C) Unlimited seat licenses.

D) Repository duplication tools.

Answer: B

Explanation: Role-based access controls and centralized management enhance collaboration security by restricting access and providing administrators with control over resources.

208. What is the primary benefit of centralized billing in GitHub Copilot Business?

A) To automate pull request approvals.

B) To consolidate team costs into a single invoice, simplifying financial management.

C) To enable unlimited repository creation.

D) To disable unused licenses automatically.

Answer: B

Explanation: Centralized billing consolidates team costs into a single invoice, simplifying financial management for organizations with multiple users.

209. How does GitHub Copilot Business support data privacy in cloud environments?

A) By automating repository duplication.

B) By encrypting all communications and adhering to privacy regulations like GDPR.

C) By storing data locally on user machines.

D) By disabling access to sensitive repositories.

Answer: B

Explanation: GitHub Copilot Business encrypts all communications and adheres to privacy regulations like GDPR, ensuring data privacy in cloud environments.

210. Which compliance requirement is addressed by GitHub Copilot Business in financial institutions?

A) Automated testing workflows.

B) Adherence to data protection standards like GDPR and ISO 27001.

C) Unlimited private repository access.

D) Role-based licensing.

Answer: B

Explanation: Adherence to data protection standards like GDPR and ISO 27001 ensures compliance for financial institutions and other regulated industries using GitHub Copilot Business.

211. What is a key benefit of using GitHub Copilot Business for large enterprises?

A) Automated code reviews.

B) Centralized tools for managing users, billing, and compliance.

C) Unlimited free seats for team members.

D) Faster repository creation.

Answer: B

Explanation: Centralized tools for managing users, billing, and compliance streamline operations for large enterprises, making GitHub Copilot Business an ideal choice for scalability.

212. Which of the following is a benefit of GitHub Copilot Business for compliance-focused teams?

A) Automated testing tools.

B) Audit logs for tracking user actions and ensuring compliance.

C) Faster repository creation.

D) Unlimited free seats for teams.

Answer: B

Explanation: Audit logs track user actions and ensure compliance, providing transparency and accountability for compliance-focused teams.

213. What is the role of Single Sign-On (SSO) in GitHub Copilot Business?

A) To automate pull request approvals.

B) To centralize user authentication through an identity provider.

C) To replace manual coding workflows with AI.

D) To enable anonymous repository access.

Answer: B

Explanation: SSO centralizes user authentication through an identity provider, enhancing security and simplifying access management for organizations.

214. How can administrators track seat usage in GitHub Copilot Business?

A) By disabling unused repositories.

B) By using centralized management tools.

C) By automating seat allocation.

D) By generating compliance reports.

Answer: B

Explanation: Centralized management tools in GitHub Copilot

Business allow administrators to track seat usage, ensuring efficient resource allocation.

215. Why is compliance important for organizations using GitHub Copilot Business?

A) To automate code reviews.

B) To meet regulatory requirements and protect sensitive data.

C) To replace manual workflows with AI tools.

D) To increase development speed.

Answer: B

Explanation: Compliance ensures organizations meet regulatory requirements and protect sensitive data, maintaining trust and legal adherence.

216. What is the purpose of role-based access controls in GitHub Copilot Business?

A) To automate testing processes.

B) To restrict access to resources based on user roles.

C) To create unlimited repositories.

D) To disable unused licenses.

Answer: B

Explanation: Role-based access controls restrict access to resources based on user roles, ensuring secure collaboration across teams.

217. How does GitHub Copilot Business ensure secure communication

in cloud-hosted environments?

A) By storing data locally on user machines.

B) By encrypting all communications and adhering to privacy standards.

C) By disabling private repositories.

D) By generating compliance certificates automatically.

Answer: B

Explanation: GitHub Copilot Business encrypts all communications and adheres to privacy standards, ensuring secure communication in cloud-hosted environments.

218. What is the primary role of centralized billing in GitHub Copilot Business?

A) To automate seat allocation.

B) To consolidate costs into a single invoice for the team.

C) To enable unlimited repository creation.

D) To generate automated compliance reports.

Answer: B

Explanation: Centralized billing consolidates costs into a single invoice for the team, simplifying financial management for organizations.

219. Which feature of GitHub Copilot Business enhances scalability for large teams?

A) Unlimited public repositories.

B) Centralized management for users, billing, and compliance.

C) Automated pull request generation.

D) Role-based licensing.

Answer: B

Explanation: Centralized management for users, billing, and compliance enhances scalability, making GitHub Copilot Business suitable for large teams.

220. What is the primary benefit of using GitHub Copilot Business in regulated industries?

A) Automated testing tools.

B) Compliance with standards like GDPR, HIPAA, and ISO 27001.

C) Unlimited repository creation.

D) Faster code generation speeds.

Answer: B

Explanation: Compliance with standards like GDPR, HIPAA, and ISO 27001 ensures GitHub Copilot Business meets the needs of regulated industries.

221. What is the primary benefit of using GitHub Copilot Business for compliance tracking?

A) Automated pull request approvals.

B) Access to audit logs for monitoring team activities and ensuring compliance.

C) Unlimited repository creation.

D) Faster code refactoring.

Answer: B

Explanation: Audit logs provide visibility into team activities, helping organizations monitor compliance with legal and regulatory standards effectively.

222. Which feature of GitHub Copilot Business improves security in multi-user environments?

A) Unlimited code generation.

B) Role-based access controls and SSO integration.

C) Faster repository duplication.

D) Automated testing workflows.

Answer: B

Explanation: Role-based access controls and SSO integration enhance security in multi-user environments by restricting access to authorized users and centralizing authentication.

223. What is the role of centralized management in GitHub Copilot Business?

A) To automate repository creation.

B) To provide a single point of control for user access, seat allocation, and billing.

C) To disable unused licenses automatically.

D) To generate automated compliance reports.

Answer: B

Explanation: Centralized management provides a single dashboard for managing user access, seat allocation, and billing, simplifying administrative tasks for organizations.

224. What is a key security feature of GitHub Copilot Enterprise?

A) Automatic repository backups.

B) Data encryption and adherence to compliance standards like GDPR.

C) Unlimited pull request approvals.

D) Automated code refactoring tools.

Answer: B

Explanation: Data encryption and adherence to compliance standards like GDPR ensure secure handling of sensitive information in GitHub Copilot Enterprise.

225. Why is GitHub Copilot Business suitable for regulated industries?

A) It provides unlimited free seats.

B) It supports compliance with standards like HIPAA, GDPR, and ISO 27001.

C) It automates pull request generation.

D) It disables private repository access.

Answer: B

Explanation: GitHub Copilot Business supports compliance with standards like HIPAA, GDPR, and ISO 27001, making it ideal for regulated industries with strict requirements.

226. What is the purpose of role-based access controls in GitHub Copilot Business?

A) To automate testing workflows.

B) To restrict access to resources based on user roles.

C) To enable anonymous repository access.

D) To simplify manual coding tasks.

Answer: B

Explanation: Role-based access controls restrict access to resources based on user roles, ensuring only authorized users can access sensitive data and repositories.

227. What is an advantage of using GitHub Copilot Business in a cloud-hosted environment?

A) Faster pull request generation.

B) Reduced dependency on local infrastructure.

C) Unlimited private repositories.

D) Automated repository backups.

Answer: B

Explanation: Using GitHub Copilot Business in a cloud-hosted environment reduces dependency on local infrastructure, enabling teams to collaborate seamlessly from anywhere.

228. How does GitHub Copilot Business support compliance audits?

A) By generating compliance certificates automatically.

B) By providing audit logs that track user activities.

C) By disabling access to all repositories during audits.

D) By automating testing workflows.

Answer: B

Explanation: GitHub Copilot Business provides audit logs that track user activities, simplifying compliance audits and ensuring transparency.

229. Which compliance framework is supported by GitHub Copilot Business?

A) DevOps pipelines.

B) GDPR, HIPAA, and ISO 27001.

C) Role-based licensing.

D) Agile Development Framework.

Answer: B

Explanation: GitHub Copilot Business supports compliance frameworks like GDPR, HIPAA, and ISO 27001, addressing the needs of regulated industries.

230. How can centralized billing in GitHub Copilot Business benefit organizations?

A) By providing unlimited free seats.

B) By consolidating all team costs into a single invoice for easy management.

C) By automating pull request approvals.

D) By generating automated compliance reports.

Answer: B

Explanation: Centralized billing consolidates team costs into a single invoice, simplifying financial management for organizations with multiple users.

231. Which feature of GitHub Copilot Business enhances scalability for large organizations?

A) Automated testing workflows.

B) Centralized management for user access, billing, and compliance.

C) Unlimited public repositories.

D) Role-based licensing.

Answer: B

Explanation: Centralized management enhances scalability by simplifying the management of user access, billing, and compliance for large organizations.

232. What is the role of SSO in GitHub Copilot Business?

A) To automate pull requests.

B) To centralize authentication through an identity provider for enhanced security.

C) To disable unused licenses automatically.

D) To enable anonymous access to repositories.

Answer: B

Explanation: SSO centralizes authentication through an identity provider like Okta or Azure AD, improving security and streamlining access management.

233. What is a key benefit of using GitHub Copilot Business for financial institutions?

A) Unlimited free seats for team members.

B) Adherence to compliance standards like GDPR and ISO 27001.

C) Faster repository creation.

D) Automated testing workflows.

Answer: B

Explanation: Adherence to compliance standards like GDPR and ISO 27001 ensures GitHub Copilot Business meets the regulatory requirements of financial institutions.

234. How does GitHub Copilot Business ensure secure collaboration across teams?

A) By automating code refactoring.

B) By integrating role-based access controls and centralized management.

C) By generating automated compliance reports.

D) By enabling anonymous repository access.

Answer: B

Explanation: Role-based access controls and centralized management ensure secure collaboration by restricting access and providing oversight of team activities.

235. Why is GitHub Copilot Business suitable for large enterprises?

A) Automated repository duplication.

B) Centralized tools for managing users, billing, and compliance.

C) Unlimited code generation.

D) Faster testing workflows.

Answer: B

Explanation: Centralized tools for managing users, billing, and compliance make GitHub Copilot Business suitable for large enterprises with complex operational needs.

236. What is the primary purpose of compliance tools in GitHub Copilot Business?

A) To automate pull request approvals.

B) To ensure adherence to industry standards and regulations.

C) To reduce development time.

D) To enable unlimited repository creation.

Answer: B

Explanation: Compliance tools in GitHub Copilot Business ensure adherence to industry standards and regulations, making it ideal for organizations in regulated industries.

237. How does GitHub Copilot Business support data privacy in self-hosted environments?

A) By encrypting all communications and adhering to privacy standards.

B) By automating repository creation.

C) By disabling private repositories.

D) By storing data locally on user devices.

Answer: A

Explanation: GitHub Copilot Business encrypts all communications and adheres to privacy standards, ensuring data privacy even in self-hosted environments.

238. What is the primary purpose of GitHub's Codeowners file?

A) To manage branch protection rules.

B) To specify individuals or teams responsible for reviewing changes in specific parts of the repository.

C) To automate the assignment of issues to team members.

D) To restrict access to repository secrets.

Answer: B

Explanation: The CODEOWNERS file specifies individuals or teams who are automatically requested for review when changes are made to certain files or directories in a repository.

Domain 5: Ethical AI Usage and Limitations

239. What is a key limitation of AI-driven tools like GitHub Copilot?

A) Lack of support for popular programming languages.

B) Inability to generate boilerplate code.

C) Potential to reflect biases in the training data.

D) Automatic approval of all pull requests.

Answer: C

Explanation: AI-driven tools like GitHub Copilot can reflect biases present in their training data. Developers must review the generated code to ensure it aligns with ethical and functional standards.

240. Why is it important to review Copilot-generated code before using it?

A) To ensure it complies with coding standards and addresses edge cases.

B) To disable automated suggestions.

C) To replace it with manually written code.

D) To ensure it contains sensitive data.

Answer: A

Explanation: Reviewing Copilot-generated code ensures it complies with coding standards, addresses edge cases, and aligns with project requirements. This prevents errors and ethical issues in the codebase.

241. What is a best practice for avoiding sensitive data exposure in Copilot suggestions?

A) Use Copilot only in public repositories.

B) Avoid including sensitive data, such as API keys, in your codebase.

C) Disable Copilot in all projects.

D) Share sensitive data in comments for clarity.

Answer: B

Explanation: Avoid including sensitive data, such as API keys or credentials, in your codebase to prevent Copilot from inadvertently using or exposing it in code suggestions.

242. What type of data is most likely to introduce biases into AI models like GitHub Copilot?

A) Data from diverse programming languages.

B) Outdated, incomplete, or biased training datasets.

C) Open-source contributions.

D) Standardized coding practices.

Answer: B

Explanation: Outdated, incomplete, or biased training datasets can introduce biases into AI models like GitHub Copilot. Developers must validate AI-generated code to mitigate these risks.

243. How can developers ensure ethical AI usage in their projects?

A) Avoid using AI tools entirely.

B) Review AI-generated code for compliance with ethical and legal standards.

C) Automate all development tasks.

D) Use AI tools without validation.

Answer: B

Explanation: Developers can ensure ethical AI usage by reviewing AI-generated code for compliance with ethical, legal, and organizational standards. Validation is critical to avoiding unintended consequences.

244. What should developers do if Copilot generates code with potential security vulnerabilities?

A) Ignore the vulnerabilities and use the code as-is.

B) Modify the code to address security vulnerabilities before using it.

C) Disable Copilot for the project.

D) Report the issue to GitHub without addressing it.

Answer: B

Explanation: Developers should modify Copilot-generated code to address any potential security vulnerabilities before using it. This ensures the safety and reliability of the application.

245. Which of the following is NOT a best practice when using GitHub Copilot?

A) Reviewing all AI-generated code.

B) Validating code against project requirements.

C) Including API keys in code for Copilot to learn from.

D) Avoiding reliance on Copilot for critical logic.

Answer: C

Explanation: Including API keys in code for Copilot to learn from is NOT a best practice. Doing so risks sensitive data exposure and violates security best practices.

246. How does the use of Copilot align with ethical AI principles?

A) By automating all coding tasks.

B) By requiring human validation to ensure fairness and accuracy.

C) By disabling manual code contributions.

D) By replacing ethical reviews with AI checks.

Answer: B

Explanation: Copilot aligns with ethical AI principles by requiring human validation to ensure fairness, accuracy, and ethical compliance in AI-generated code.

247. Why is it important to validate Copilot-generated code for regulatory compliance?

A) To ensure it meets legal requirements for the industry or region.

B) To automatically approve pull requests.

C) To disable manual coding workflows.

D) To reduce development time.

Answer: A

Explanation: Validating Copilot-generated code ensures it meets legal and regulatory requirements for the industry or region, avoiding potential legal or compliance issues.

248. What is a potential ethical risk of relying solely on Copilot for code generation?

A) Reduced development speed.

B) Lack of diversity in code patterns and solutions.

C) Automatic fixing of all bugs.

D) Increased manual review time.

Answer: B

Explanation: Relying solely on Copilot for code generation can lead to a lack of diversity in code patterns and solutions, reflecting biases in its training data.

249. What should developers do if Copilot generates code that violates copyright?

A) Use the code without modifications.

B) Replace the code with an original implementation.

C) Ignore the copyright violation.

D) Report the issue to GitHub.

Answer: B

Explanation: If Copilot generates code that violates copyright, developers should replace it with an original implementation to avoid legal and ethical issues.

250. How can developers minimize the risk of AI biases in Copilot-generated code?

A) Avoid using AI tools altogether.

B) Conduct thorough code reviews and validation.

C) Use Copilot only for small projects.

D) Enable Copilot in all repositories without restrictions.

Answer: B

Explanation: Conducting thorough code reviews and validation helps minimize the risk of AI biases in Copilot-generated code, ensuring it meets ethical and project standards.

251. Which of the following actions aligns with ethical AI usage?

A) Sharing sensitive data in public repositories.

B) Validating AI-generated code for security vulnerabilities.

C) Automating all code reviews.

D) Ignoring potential biases in AI suggestions.

Answer: B

Explanation: Validating AI-generated code for security vulnerabilities aligns with ethical AI usage, ensuring safe and responsible implementation of AI-driven tools.

252. How does Copilot handle sensitive data in private repositories?

A) It disables suggestions for private repositories.

B) It does not store or retain private code, ensuring data privacy.

C) It shares data with public repositories.

D) It automatically encrypts all suggestions.

Answer: B

Explanation: Copilot does not store or retain private code, ensuring data privacy and security for private repositories.

253. What is a key ethical consideration when using AI tools like Copilot for development?

A) Automating all development tasks.

B) Reviewing AI-generated code for ethical, security, and legal compliance.

C) Disabling AI tools for all projects.

D) Relying solely on AI tools without validation.

Answer: B

Explanation: Reviewing AI-generated code for ethical, security, and legal compliance is a key consideration when using AI tools like Copilot, ensuring responsible usage.

254. Why is it important to avoid including sensitive data in comments or code?

A) To prevent exposing it in Copilot-generated suggestions.

B) To reduce comment clutter.

C) To disable Copilot functionality.

D) To simplify code reviews.

Answer: A

Explanation: Avoiding sensitive data in comments or code prevents it from being exposed in Copilot-generated suggestions, ensuring data security and privacy.

255. What should developers do if they suspect bias in Copilot-generated code?

A) Ignore the bias and use the code as-is.

B) Validate and modify the code to address the bias.

C) Disable Copilot for the project.

D) Report the bias to GitHub without addressing it.

Answer: B

Explanation: Developers should validate and modify Copilot-generated code to address any suspected bias, ensuring fairness and accuracy.

256. How can developers ensure fairness in Copilot-generated code?

A) Automate all code reviews.

B) Conduct thorough validation and testing for diverse use cases.

C) Disable Copilot for critical projects.

D) Use Copilot without reviewing the suggestions.

Answer: B

Explanation: Conducting thorough validation and testing for diverse use cases ensures fairness in Copilot-generated code, reducing the impact of biases.

257. What is a best practice for using Copilot ethically in collaborative projects?

A) Reviewing all AI-generated code as a team.

B) Disabling Copilot for all collaborators.

C) Automating all pull requests.

D) Sharing sensitive data for training purposes.

Answer: A

Explanation: Reviewing all AI-generated code as a team ensures ethical usage of Copilot in collaborative projects, maintaining code quality and compliance.

258. Which of the following is NOT a limitation of GitHub Copilot?

A) Reflecting biases in training data.

B) Generating incomplete or context-dependent suggestions.

C) Automatically validating all generated code.

D) Lacking understanding of project-specific requirements.

Answer: C

Explanation: GitHub Copilot does NOT automatically validate all generated code. Validation must be performed by developers to ensure accuracy and compliance.

259. How can developers ensure Copilot-generated code aligns with ethical standards?

A) Use Copilot only in private repositories.

B) Review and validate all generated code before using it.

C) Enable automatic code merging.

D) Avoid using comments in their code.

Answer: B

Explanation: Developers must review and validate all Copilot-generated code to ensure it aligns with ethical standards, project requirements, and security guidelines.

260. What is the potential risk of using Copilot in collaborative projects?

A) Reduced coding speed.

B) Propagation of biased or insecure code across the team.

C) Automatic disabling of manual workflows.

D) Lack of collaboration features.

Answer: B

Explanation: Using Copilot in collaborative projects without proper validation can propagate biased or insecure code, impacting the entire team's work and project integrity.

261. Which of the following is NOT an ethical consideration when using GitHub Copilot?

A) Ensuring generated code is free from security vulnerabilities.

B) Validating code for compliance with legal and regulatory standards.

C) Relying on Copilot for all project-critical logic without manual review.

D) Avoiding sensitive data in code and comments.

Answer: C

Explanation: Relying on Copilot for all project-critical logic without manual review is NOT an ethical consideration. Developers must validate all generated code to ensure its accuracy and safety.

262. Why is it important to avoid over-reliance on GitHub Copilot for critical functionality?

A) To ensure compliance with licensing terms.

B) Because Copilot may generate incomplete or context-dependent code.

C) To reduce project costs.

D) Because Copilot cannot handle large projects.

Answer: B

Explanation: Over-reliance on Copilot for critical functionality is risky because it may generate incomplete or context-dependent code. Developers should validate and refine suggestions.

263. What is a potential ethical issue with using AI-generated code in sensitive applications?

A) Reduced code readability.

B) Introduction of biases or errors that could have harmful consequences.

C) Delayed development timelines.

D) Increased collaboration overhead.

Answer: B

Explanation: Using AI-generated code in sensitive applications can introduce biases or errors that may lead to harmful consequences if not carefully reviewed and tested.

264. What is the role of developers in mitigating AI biases in Copilot suggestions?

A) Avoid using AI tools entirely.

B) Conduct thorough reviews and modify biased code as needed.

C) Automate the review process.

D) Use Copilot only for minor tasks.

Answer: B

Explanation: Developers play a crucial role in mitigating AI biases by conducting thorough reviews and modifying problematic code to ensure fairness and accuracy.

265. How should sensitive information, such as API keys, be handled in Copilot-assisted projects?

A) Include them in comments for clarity.

B) Store them securely outside the codebase.

C) Share them with collaborators for better suggestions.

D) Embed them directly in the code for Copilot to learn.

Answer: B

Explanation: Sensitive information like API keys should be stored securely outside the codebase to prevent exposure in Copilot-generated suggestions or shared repositories.

266. What is a key ethical consideration when using Copilot for open-source projects?

A) Ensuring the generated code adheres to the project's licensing terms.

B) Avoiding the use of public repositories.

C) Disabling Copilot for sensitive projects.

D) Automatically merging all pull requests.

Answer: A

Explanation: When using Copilot for open-source projects, it is essential to ensure the generated code adheres to the project's licensing terms to avoid legal and ethical issues.

267. How can developers verify the accuracy of Copilot-generated code?

A) Use automated testing tools and manual reviews.

B) Enable Copilot's auto-validation feature.

C) Avoid using the generated code entirely.

D) Share the code with external reviewers.

Answer: A

Explanation: Developers can verify the accuracy of Copilot-generated code by using automated testing tools and conducting manual reviews to ensure it meets project requirements.

268. Why is it important to test Copilot-generated code for edge cases?

A) To ensure the code is readable.

B) To validate its behavior in uncommon or extreme scenarios.

C) To reduce the time spent on manual reviews.

D) To simplify code refactoring.

Answer: B

Explanation: Testing Copilot-generated code for edge cases validates its behavior in uncommon or extreme scenarios, ensuring it functions correctly under all conditions.

269. What is the role of ethical AI guidelines in using Copilot?

A) To automate all coding tasks.

B) To ensure responsible usage of AI for secure and fair development.

C) To replace human developers with AI-generated code.

D) To disable Copilot for certain repositories.

Answer: B

Explanation: Ethical AI guidelines ensure responsible usage of AI tools like Copilot, promoting secure, fair, and unbiased development practices.

270. What should developers do if Copilot generates potentially illegal code snippets?

A) Use the code without validation.

B) Replace it with compliant alternatives.

C) Report the issue to GitHub and ignore it.

D) Disable Copilot for the project.

Answer: B

Explanation: If Copilot generates potentially illegal code snippets, developers should replace them with compliant alternatives to avoid legal and ethical issues.

271. Which of the following is a limitation of AI-driven code generation?

A) Lack of support for common programming languages.

B) Inability to adapt to specific project requirements without context.

C) Automatic testing of all generated code.

D) Disabling manual coding tasks.

Answer: B

Explanation: AI-driven code generation, including Copilot, cannot fully adapt to specific project requirements without sufficient context from the developer.

272. Why is it important to document the use of AI-generated code in projects?

A) To simplify future debugging and compliance reviews.

B) To reduce the workload on collaborators.

C) To automate testing workflows.

D) To ensure compatibility with open-source licenses.

Answer: A

Explanation: Documenting the use of AI-generated code simplifies future debugging and compliance reviews, providing transparency and accountability.

273. How can teams ensure ethical AI usage when collaborating on Copilot-assisted projects?

A) Avoid using Copilot altogether.

B) Establish clear guidelines for reviewing and validating suggestions.

C) Automate all pull requests.

D) Rely solely on Copilot for critical logic.

Answer: B

Explanation: Teams can ensure ethical AI usage by establishing clear guidelines for reviewing and validating Copilot-generated suggestions to maintain code quality and compliance.

274. What is a potential risk of not validating Copilot-generated code?

A) Reduced collaboration efficiency.

B) Introduction of errors, security vulnerabilities, or biases in the codebase.

C) Increased development costs.

D) Lack of support for open-source projects.

Answer: B

Explanation: Not validating Copilot-generated code can introduce errors, security vulnerabilities, or biases, potentially compromising the project's integrity and safety.

275. Which of the following aligns with responsible AI usage in software development?

A) Automating all testing and validation tasks.

B) Regularly reviewing AI-generated code for biases and security issues.

C) Disabling AI tools for complex projects.

D) Replacing all manual coding workflows with AI-generated code.

Answer: B

Explanation: Regularly reviewing AI-generated code for biases and security issues aligns with responsible AI usage, ensuring safe and ethical development practices.

276. Why is it important to avoid sharing sensitive data in public repositories when using Copilot?

A) To reduce repository size.

B) To prevent sensitive data from being used in AI-generated suggestions.

C) To simplify debugging and refactoring.

D) To ensure faster code completion.

Answer: B

Explanation: Avoiding sensitive data in public repositories prevents it from being used in AI-generated suggestions, protecting privacy and security.

277. What should developers do if Copilot generates biased or unfair code?

A) Use the code without modifications.

B) Modify the code to ensure fairness and report the issue if necessary.

C) Ignore the biased code and disable Copilot.

D) Share the biased code with collaborators.

Answer: B

Explanation: Developers should modify Copilot-generated code to ensure fairness and report biases to GitHub if necessary, promoting ethical AI usage.

278. How can developers promote inclusivity when using AI tools like Copilot?

A) Avoid using Copilot for large projects.

B) Validate code for fairness and test it in diverse scenarios.

C) Rely on AI tools for all coding tasks.

D) Use Copilot only for individual projects.

Answer: B

Explanation: Promoting inclusivity involves validating Copilot-generated code for fairness and testing it in diverse scenarios to ensure it meets the needs of all users.

279. What should developers do if Copilot generates code that violates legal licensing terms?

A) Use the code as-is since it was AI-generated.

B) Replace the code with an original implementation that adheres to licensing terms.

C) Share the code publicly to gather feedback.

D) Report the issue but continue using the code.

Answer: B

Explanation: If Copilot generates code that violates licensing terms, developers must replace it with an original implementation to avoid legal and ethical issues.

280. How can teams ensure sensitive client data is not exposed in Copilot-generated code?

A) Avoid using sensitive data in the codebase altogether.

B) Encrypt sensitive data directly in the codebase.

C) Use Copilot only for public projects.

D) Share sensitive data in comments for better suggestions.

Answer: A

Explanation: Sensitive client data should not be included in the codebase to ensure it is not exposed in Copilot-generated suggestions or shared repositories.

281. What is a key step for ensuring AI-generated code aligns with industry standards?

A) Enable Copilot auto-validation.

B) Conduct manual code reviews against industry standards.

C) Use Copilot exclusively for testing purposes.

D) Avoid using AI tools in regulated industries.

Answer: B

Explanation: Manual code reviews are essential to ensure AI-generated code aligns with industry standards, especially in regulated industries.

282. What is a limitation of Copilot when generating code for ethical decision-making systems?

A) It cannot generate any code for such systems.

B) It lacks contextual understanding of ethical trade-offs.

C) It automatically disables suggestions for sensitive code.

D) It only supports procedural programming.

Answer: B

Explanation: Copilot lacks the contextual understanding required to address ethical trade-offs in decision-making systems, making manual validation critical.

283. What should developers do to reduce potential misuse of Copilot-generated code?

A) Share all generated code publicly for review.

B) Test and validate code for ethical and security compliance.

C) Use Copilot only in private repositories.

D) Avoid using Copilot for critical applications.

Answer: B

Explanation: Testing and validating Copilot-generated code ensures it meets ethical and security compliance, reducing the risk of misuse.

284. Why is it important to validate the ethical implications of AI-generated code in health-related applications?

A) To ensure faster code execution.

B) To avoid harming users or violating regulations like HIPAA.

C) To reduce debugging time.

D) To simplify testing workflows.

Answer: B

Explanation: Validating AI-generated code in health-related applications prevents harm to users and ensures compliance with regulations like HIPAA.

285. What is the primary risk of exposing proprietary algorithms in Copilot-assisted projects?

A) Increased collaboration time.

B) Loss of intellectual property or competitive advantage.

C) Reduced readability of the algorithm.

D) Slower code generation speeds.

Answer: B

Explanation: Exposing proprietary algorithms risks losing intellectual property or competitive advantage, making it essential to secure sensitive code.

286. How can developers reduce the risk of introducing biases in Copilot-generated machine learning code?

A) Avoid using Copilot for machine learning projects.

B) Validate the code and datasets for fairness and inclusivity.

C) Use only pre-trained models suggested by Copilot.

D) Automate all code reviews.

Answer: B

Explanation: Developers must validate code and datasets for fairness and inclusivity to reduce the risk of introducing biases in machine learning projects.

287. What is the role of transparency in ethical AI usage?

A) To automate all compliance processes.

B) To document and communicate the use of AI in development projects.

C) To replace manual validation workflows.

D) To reduce project timelines.

Answer: B

Explanation: Transparency involves documenting and communicating the use of AI in development projects, building trust and accountability in ethical AI usage.

288. How can developers ensure Copilot-generated code adheres to company policies?

A) Automate pull request approvals for all suggestions.

B) Review and test generated code against company policies and standards.

C) Use Copilot only for non-critical tasks.

D) Disable Copilot for internal projects.

Answer: B

Explanation: Reviewing and testing Copilot-generated code ensures it adheres to company policies and standards, maintaining compliance.

289. What is the ethical concern of using Copilot-generated code from open-source projects without attribution?

A) It violates licensing requirements and disrespects the original authors.

B) It increases project costs.

C) It reduces the readability of the code.

D) It slows down development timelines.

Answer: A

Explanation: Using Copilot-generated code from open-source projects without attribution violates licensing requirements and disrespects the original authors' contributions.

290. Why is it important to educate team members about AI biases in Copilot?

A) To increase their coding speed.

B) To prepare them for validating and mitigating biases in suggestions.

C) To replace manual workflows with AI-generated code.

D) To automate compliance reviews.

Answer: B

Explanation: Educating team members about AI biases prepares them for validating and mitigating biases in Copilot-generated suggestions, ensuring ethical practices.

291. How can developers avoid unintentional plagiarism with Copilot-generated code?

A) Avoid using Copilot for large projects.

B) Validate the originality of the code and provide proper attribution when required.

C) Use Copilot exclusively for testing purposes.

D) Automate all code reviews.

Answer: B

Explanation: Validating the originality of Copilot-generated code and providing proper attribution prevents unintentional plagiarism and legal issues.

292. What is the ethical concern of using Copilot for generating discriminatory algorithms?

A) Reduced debugging time.

B) Potential harm to users and violation of fairness principles.

C) Increased collaboration overhead.

D) Limited applicability of the algorithm.

Answer: B

Explanation: Using Copilot to generate discriminatory algorithms can harm users and violate fairness principles, making it unethical and unacceptable.

293. Why is it important to validate Copilot-generated code in financial applications?

A) To reduce debugging time.

B) To ensure compliance with financial regulations and prevent errors.

C) To enable faster code execution.

D) To simplify coding workflows.

Answer: B

Explanation: Validating Copilot-generated code in financial applications ensures compliance with financial regulations and prevents errors that could have significant consequences.

294. What is the primary risk of relying on Copilot for security-sensitive code?

A) Reduced collaboration efficiency.

B) Introduction of vulnerabilities that may be exploited by attackers.

C) Increased development time.

D) Limited support for advanced algorithms.

Answer: B

Explanation: Relying on Copilot for security-sensitive code without validation can introduce vulnerabilities that attackers may exploit, compromising the application's security.

295. How can organizations promote ethical AI usage in their development teams?

A) Automate all testing and validation tasks.

B) Develop guidelines for reviewing and validating AI-generated code.

C) Replace manual coding workflows with AI-generated code.

D) Disable Copilot for high-priority projects.

Answer: B

Explanation: Organizations can promote ethical AI usage by developing guidelines for reviewing and validating AI-generated code, ensuring responsibility and fairness.

296. What is the role of documentation in ethical AI usage?

A) To automate compliance processes.

B) To provide transparency and accountability in AI-assisted projects.

C) To replace manual workflows with AI tools.

D) To reduce project timelines.

Answer: B

Explanation: Documentation provides transparency and accountability in AI-assisted projects, ensuring ethical practices and building trust.

297. Why is it important to test Copilot-generated code in mission-critical systems?

A) To reduce the time spent on manual reviews.

B) To ensure reliability, safety, and compliance with standards.

C) To increase the speed of code generation.

D) To simplify debugging workflows.

Answer: B

Explanation: Testing Copilot-generated code in mission-critical systems ensures reliability, safety, and compliance with industry standards, preventing failures.

298. Which of the following is a best practice for using Copilot in sensitive industries like healthcare?

A) Automate all code approvals.

B) Validate generated code for compliance with security and privacy regulations.

C) Use Copilot exclusively for non-sensitive projects.

D) Avoid using AI tools in such industries.

Answer: B

Explanation: Validating Copilot-generated code for compliance with security and privacy regulations is a best practice for its ethical use in sensitive industries like healthcare.

299. How can developers use Copilot Chat to explore alternative solutions for a function?

A) Ask specific questions about alternative approaches.

B) Disable the function and rewrite it manually.

C) Use external debugging tools.

D) Automatically rewrite the function.

Answer: A

Explanation: Developers can ask specific questions about alternative approaches in Copilot Chat to explore different ways of implementing a function. This fosters creativity and flexibility in coding.

Domain 6: Productivity and Collaboration

300. How can GitHub Copilot enhance team collaboration in a multi-developer project?

A) By replacing code reviews.

B) By providing consistent code suggestions across the team.

C) By automating repository creation.

D) By disabling non-critical repositories.

Answer: B

Explanation: GitHub Copilot enhances collaboration by providing consistent code suggestions, ensuring that all team members follow similar coding patterns and maintain code quality.

301. Which GitHub Copilot feature allows developers to experiment with new workflows?

A) Copilot Business

B) GitHub Copilot Labs

C) Centralized Billing

D) Multi-Factor Authentication (MFA)

Answer: B

Explanation: GitHub Copilot Labs provides experimental features and workflows, enabling developers to explore new ways of enhancing productivity and collaboration.

302. How does Copilot improve productivity in multi-language projects?

A) By supporting only one programming language at a time.

B) By providing context-aware suggestions for multiple languages in the same codebase.

C) By disabling suggestions for rarely used languages.

D) By automating language-specific testing.

Answer: B

Explanation: Copilot improves productivity in multi-language projects by providing context-aware suggestions for multiple languages, helping developers work efficiently across diverse codebases.

303. What is the role of feedback in improving Copilot's suggestions?

A) To automatically adapt Copilot to all projects.

B) To help refine its machine learning models based on user input.

C) To disable irrelevant suggestions permanently.

D) To enable auto-approval of pull requests.

Answer: B

Explanation: User feedback helps refine Copilot's machine learning models, improving the relevance and accuracy of its suggestions over time.

304. Which feature of GitHub Copilot supports rapid prototyping in collaborative projects?

A) Automated pull request approvals

B) Context-aware code suggestions

C) Centralized billing

D) Role-based access controls

Answer: B

Explanation: Context-aware code suggestions enable rapid prototyping by helping developers quickly implement ideas and iterate on them in collaborative projects.

305. What is a key benefit of using Copilot in large codebases?

A) It disables unused repositories.

B) It helps developers quickly navigate and understand unfamiliar code.

C) It automates repository duplication.

D) It generates compliance reports.

Answer: B

Explanation: Copilot helps developers quickly navigate and understand unfamiliar code in large codebases by providing relevant suggestions and explanations.

306. How does GitHub Copilot assist in resolving merge conflicts during collaboration?

A) By automating conflict resolution without developer input.

B) By suggesting context-aware changes to resolve conflicts.

C) By disabling conflicting files.

D) By merging all changes automatically.

Answer: B

Explanation: GitHub Copilot assists in resolving merge conflicts by suggesting context-aware changes, helping developers address issues efficiently.

307. What is the primary purpose of GitHub Copilot Labs?

A) To replace manual testing workflows.

B) To introduce experimental features for improving developer productivity.

C) To disable non-essential repositories.

D) To automate billing and seat allocation.

Answer: B

Explanation: GitHub Copilot Labs introduces experimental features designed to enhance developer productivity and explore innovative workflows.

308. Why is Copilot particularly useful in collaborative projects with diverse skill levels?

A) It automates all manual coding tasks.

B) It provides learning opportunities by explaining suggestions and code snippets.

C) It disables advanced features for less experienced developers.

D) It generates compliance certificates.

Answer: B

Explanation: Copilot is useful in collaborative projects with diverse skill levels as it provides learning opportunities by explaining suggestions and code snippets, helping less experienced developers grow.

309. How can teams use GitHub Copilot to maintain consistent coding practices?

A) By automating pull request reviews.

B) By using Copilot's suggestions to enforce style and structure guidelines.

C) By disabling Copilot for custom projects.

D) By replacing code reviews with AI-generated reports.

Answer: B

Explanation: Teams can use Copilot's suggestions to enforce consistent style and structure guidelines, ensuring uniformity across the codebase.

310. What is a productivity benefit of using Copilot in large projects with legacy code?

A) It disables legacy code for better performance.

B) It helps identify patterns and provides intelligent suggestions for modifying legacy code.

C) It automates repository migration.

D) It generates compliance reports for older code.

Answer: B

Explanation: Copilot identifies patterns in legacy code and provides intelligent suggestions, aiding developers in modifying and modernizing older codebases.

311. Which GitHub Copilot feature allows developers to provide direct feedback on suggestions?

A) Centralized Billing

B) Suggestion Feedback Mechanism

C) Role-Based Access Controls

D) SSO Integration

Answer: B

Explanation: The Suggestion Feedback Mechanism allows developers to provide direct feedback on Copilot's suggestions, helping improve its accuracy and relevance.

312. How does Copilot assist in projects that use multiple frameworks?

A) By disabling suggestions for less common frameworks.

B) By providing context-aware suggestions tailored to the frameworks used.

C) By automating framework-specific testing workflows.

D) By replacing framework documentation with code snippets.

Answer: B

Explanation: Copilot provides context-aware suggestions tailored to the frameworks used, enabling developers to work seamlessly across multiple frameworks in a single project.

313. What role does GitHub Copilot Labs play in multi-language projects?

A) It disables less commonly used languages.

B) It experiments with advanced multi-language support features.

C) It generates compliance reports for each language.

D) It automates translation of code between languages.

Answer: B

Explanation: GitHub Copilot Labs experiments with advanced multi-language support features, enhancing productivity for developers working in diverse codebases.

314. How can feedback loops improve Copilot suggestions in collaborative projects?

A) By automating pull request reviews.

B) By learning from user inputs and refining its suggestions.

C) By disabling irrelevant suggestions permanently.

D) By generating detailed compliance reports for each suggestion.

Answer: B

Explanation: Feedback loops allow Copilot to learn from user inputs, refining its suggestions to better suit the needs of collaborative projects.

315. What is a key advantage of using Copilot in large, distributed teams?

A) It replaces manual code reviews.

B) It ensures consistent coding patterns across geographically dispersed teams.

C) It automates repository creation and management.

D) It generates compliance certificates for all contributors.

Answer: B

Explanation: Copilot ensures consistent coding patterns across geographically dispersed teams by providing standardized suggestions and maintaining code quality.

316. Which GitHub Copilot feature supports onboarding new developers to a project?

A) Automated pull request approvals

B) Contextual code suggestions and explanations

C) Centralized billing

D) Role-based licensing

Answer: B

Explanation: Copilot supports onboarding new developers by providing contextual code suggestions and explanations, helping them quickly understand the codebase and contribute effectively.

317. How does GitHub Copilot enhance productivity in projects with rapidly changing requirements?

A) By automating repository duplication.

B) By providing quick, context-aware suggestions for adapting to new requirements.

C) By disabling outdated code suggestions.

D) By automating compliance reviews.

Answer: B

Explanation: Copilot enhances productivity by providing quick, context-aware suggestions, enabling developers to adapt to rapidly changing requirements efficiently.

318. What is a key benefit of GitHub Copilot Labs for developers exploring new technologies?

A) It automates repository migration.

B) It provides experimental features that help developers test and learn new technologies.

C) It disables non-critical repositories.

D) It generates compliance reports for experimental projects.

Answer: B

Explanation: GitHub Copilot Labs provides experimental features, enabling developers to test and learn new technologies while exploring innovative workflows.

319. How can developers use Copilot to improve productivity in code review processes?

A) By automating all review tasks.

B) By using Copilot's suggestions to identify potential issues and improve code quality.

C) By replacing manual reviews with AI-generated reports.

D) By disabling irrelevant pull requests.

Answer: B

Explanation: Copilot's suggestions help developers identify potential issues and improve code quality, streamlining the code review process.

320. Which GitHub Copilot feature is most useful for team brainstorming?

A) Context-aware code suggestions.

B) Automated pull request approvals.

C) Repository duplication tools.

D) Centralized billing.

Answer: A

Explanation: Context-aware code suggestions allow teams to brainstorm ideas by quickly prototyping code snippets and exploring different solutions collaboratively.

321. What is the benefit of Copilot in projects with frequent code refactoring?

A) It disables unused code.

B) It provides suggestions that align with the refactored code structure.

C) It automates repository duplication.

D) It generates compliance reports.

Answer: B

Explanation: Copilot provides suggestions that align with the refactored code structure, helping developers maintain consistency and avoid errors during frequent updates.

322. How can Copilot improve collaboration in cross-functional teams?

A) By automating all manual tasks.

B) By providing explanations for code suggestions that help non-technical members understand the logic.

C) By disabling access for non-developers.

D) By generating compliance certificates.

Answer: B

Explanation: Copilot improves collaboration in cross-functional teams by providing explanations for code suggestions, making it easier for non-technical members to understand and contribute.

323. Which experimental feature in GitHub Copilot Labs supports code translation?

A) Code Explanation

B) Code Transformation

C) Multi-Language Support

D) Feedback Mechanism

Answer: B

Explanation: The Code Transformation feature in GitHub Copilot Labs supports translating code between different programming languages, enhancing productivity in diverse projects.

324. How can Copilot help teams identify potential bottlenecks in their codebase?

A) By automating pull request approvals.

B) By suggesting optimizations for slow or inefficient code.

C) By disabling non-critical repositories.

D) By generating automated compliance reports.

Answer: B

Explanation: Copilot suggests optimizations for slow or inefficient code, helping teams identify and resolve potential bottlenecks in their codebase.

325. What is a key use case for GitHub Copilot in pair programming?

A) Automating code reviews.

B) Providing real-time suggestions to complement the work of both developers.

C) Replacing one of the developers in the pair.

D) Disabling manual coding workflows.

Answer: B

Explanation: In pair programming, Copilot provides real-time suggestions, complementing the work of both developers and enhancing collaboration.

326. Which GitHub Copilot Labs feature can help developers simplify complex code?

A) Code Simplification

B) Code Explanation

C) Pull Request Automation

D) Role-Based Licensing

Answer: B

Explanation: The Code Explanation feature in GitHub Copilot Labs helps developers simplify and understand complex code, improving readability and maintainability.

327. How can Copilot enhance collaboration during code reviews?

A) By generating compliance reports.

B) By providing alternative solutions to improve the reviewed code.

C) By disabling irrelevant pull requests.

D) By automating repository creation.

Answer: B

Explanation: Copilot enhances collaboration during code reviews by suggesting alternative solutions, helping reviewers improve the quality of the code.

328. What is a productivity advantage of using Copilot in documentation-heavy projects?

A) It disables irrelevant documentation files.

B) It generates boilerplate documentation based on code context.

C) It automates compliance checks for documentation.

D) It replaces manual documentation entirely.

Answer: B

Explanation: Copilot generates boilerplate documentation based on code context, saving time and improving productivity in documentation-heavy projects.

329. How does Copilot improve the onboarding process for new developers?

A) By automating repository setup.

B) By providing contextual suggestions and explanations for the existing codebase.

C) By disabling complex features temporarily.

D) By generating compliance reports automatically.

Answer: B

Explanation: Copilot provides contextual suggestions and explanations, helping new developers quickly understand the codebase and contribute effectively.

330. Which GitHub Copilot feature supports experimenting with alternative coding approaches?

A) Feedback Mechanism

B) Code Exploration in Copilot Labs

C) Automated Testing Workflows

D) Centralized Billing

Answer: B

Explanation: The Code Exploration feature in Copilot Labs enables developers to experiment with alternative coding approaches, fostering innovation and creativity.

331. How can Copilot assist in debugging collaborative projects?

A) By automating all testing workflows.

B) By suggesting potential fixes for identified errors.

C) By disabling irrelevant lines of code.

D) By generating compliance certificates.

Answer: B

Explanation: Copilot assists in debugging by suggesting potential fixes for identified errors, helping teams resolve issues faster in collaborative projects.

332. What is a key benefit of using Copilot in agile development workflows?

A) It disables unused repositories.

B) It adapts to rapid iterations by providing context-aware, real-time suggestions.

C) It automates pull request approvals.

D) It replaces manual coding entirely.

Answer: B

Explanation: Copilot adapts to rapid iterations in agile workflows by providing context-aware, real-time suggestions, enhancing flexibility and productivity.

333. How does GitHub Copilot Labs support developer education?

A) By automating code generation for all projects.

B) By offering features like Code Explanation to help developers learn new concepts.

C) By disabling advanced features temporarily.

D) By generating compliance reports for learning projects.

Answer: B

Explanation: GitHub Copilot Labs supports developer education by offering features like Code Explanation, which helps developers understand and learn new concepts effectively.

334. Which Copilot feature can help teams adhere to coding standards in multi-developer projects?

A) Role-Based Licensing

B) Consistent Code Suggestions

C) Automated Repository Duplication

D) Feedback Mechanism

Answer: B

Explanation: Consistent code suggestions ensure that all developers follow the same coding standards, maintaining quality in multi-developer projects.

335. What is a key benefit of the feedback mechanism in GitHub Copilot?

A) It automates pull request approvals.

B) It allows developers to refine Copilot's suggestions based on team needs.

C) It disables irrelevant features automatically.

D) It generates compliance certifications.

Answer: B

Explanation: The feedback mechanism allows developers to refine Copilot's suggestions, improving its relevance and usefulness for team-specific needs.

336. How does GitHub Copilot support multilingual teams?

A) By disabling less common languages.

B) By providing context-aware suggestions for multiple programming languages.

C) By automating language translation workflows.

D) By generating compliance reports for language-specific projects.

Answer: B

Explanation: Copilot supports multilingual teams by providing context-aware suggestions for multiple programming languages, enabling seamless collaboration across diverse teams.

337. What is the role of experimental features in GitHub Copilot Labs?

A) To automate repository creation.

B) To introduce new tools for improving productivity and collaboration.

C) To disable unused features temporarily.

D) To replace manual workflows with AI-driven processes.

Answer: B

Explanation: Experimental features in GitHub Copilot Labs introduce new tools for improving productivity and collaboration, allowing developers to explore innovative workflows.

337. Which Copilot feature can help teams identify redundant code?

A) Automated Testing Tools

B) Code Simplification in GitHub Copilot Labs

C) Feedback Mechanism

D) Multi-Language Support

Answer: B

Explanation: The Code Simplification feature in GitHub Copilot Labs helps teams identify and eliminate redundant code, improving efficiency and maintainability.

338. What is a key advantage of using Copilot in cross-team collaborations?

A) It disables irrelevant repositories.

B) It ensures consistent coding practices across different teams.

C) It automates all manual coding tasks.

D) It generates compliance reports for inter-team projects.

Answer: B

Explanation: Copilot ensures consistent coding practices across different teams, promoting efficiency and collaboration in cross-team projects.

339. How does GitHub Copilot assist in reducing technical debt in collaborative projects?

A) By generating compliance certificates.

B) By suggesting efficient and maintainable code solutions.

C) By automating pull request approvals.

D) By disabling unused repositories.

Answer: B

Explanation: Copilot helps reduce technical debt by providing code suggestions that are efficient, maintainable, and aligned with best practices.

340. What is the role of feedback in enhancing GitHub Copilot Labs features?

A) To automate testing workflows.

B) To help refine experimental features based on developer input.

C) To generate compliance reports for experimental projects.

D) To disable irrelevant features.

Answer: B

Explanation: Feedback from developers helps refine experimental features in GitHub Copilot Labs, ensuring they meet user needs and improve over time.

341. How does Copilot support collaboration in asynchronous development workflows?

A) By automating repository duplication.

B) By providing consistent suggestions across different time zones and team members.

C) By disabling conflicting pull requests.

D) By generating compliance reports for asynchronous tasks.

Answer: B

Explanation: Copilot supports asynchronous workflows by providing consistent suggestions, enabling seamless collaboration across different time zones and team members.

342. Which GitHub Copilot Labs feature helps developers understand legacy code?

A) Pull Request Automation

B) Code Explanation

C) Code Simplification

D) Feedback Mechanism

Answer: B

Explanation: The Code Explanation feature in GitHub Copilot Labs helps developers understand legacy code by providing detailed explanations of its purpose and functionality.

343. How can Copilot improve productivity during sprint planning?

A) By automating all sprint tasks.

B) By helping estimate effort through prototyping and code snippet suggestions.

C) By generating compliance reports for sprint goals.

D) By replacing manual planning with AI-driven workflows.

Answer: B

Explanation: Copilot improves productivity during sprint planning by helping estimate effort through quick prototyping and relevant code snippet suggestions.

344. What is a key productivity feature of Copilot for projects with frequent API updates?

A) It disables outdated API calls.

B) It suggests updated syntax and usage for changing APIs.

C) It automates API documentation generation.

D) It replaces API testing with AI-driven workflows.

Answer: B

Explanation: Copilot suggests updated syntax and usage for changing APIs, helping developers quickly adapt to updates and maintain productivity.

345. How does Copilot facilitate code reuse in large teams?

A) By disabling redundant code snippets.

B) By suggesting reusable patterns and functions based on project context.

C) By automating repository duplication for shared modules.

D) By replacing manual code reuse workflows.

Answer: B

Explanation: Copilot facilitates code reuse by suggesting reusable patterns and functions based on the project's context, promoting efficiency in large teams.

346. Which GitHub Copilot feature is most useful for identifying security vulnerabilities in code?

A) Code Simplification

B) Context-Aware Suggestions

C) Security Auditing (Experimental in Labs)

D) Automated Pull Request Approvals

Answer: C

Explanation: The Security Auditing feature (experimental in GitHub Copilot Labs) helps identify potential security vulnerabilities and suggests fixes.

347. What is the benefit of Copilot's multi-language support in global teams?

A) It disables less commonly used languages.

B) It enables seamless collaboration by providing accurate suggestions for multiple languages.

C) It automates language translation workflows.

D) It generates compliance reports for language-based projects.

Answer: B

Explanation: Multi-language support enables seamless collaboration in global teams by providing accurate, context-aware suggestions for multiple languages.

348. How does Copilot assist in maintaining project documentation?

A) By automating all documentation tasks.

B) By generating relevant documentation snippets based on the codebase.

C) By disabling irrelevant documentation files.

D) By replacing manual documentation workflows entirely.

Answer: B

Explanation: Copilot generates relevant documentation snippets based on the codebase, helping developers maintain accurate and up-to-date documentation.

349. How can Copilot help teams adhere to deadlines in tight schedules?

A) By automating repository creation.

B) By providing quick and accurate code suggestions to speed up development.

C) By replacing manual coding workflows entirely.

D) By generating compliance reports for faster reviews.

Answer: B

Explanation: Copilot helps teams adhere to deadlines by providing quick and accurate code suggestions, speeding up development without sacrificing quality.

350. What is the advantage of using Copilot for testing-related tasks?

A) It disables irrelevant testing files.

B) It suggests boilerplate testing code for various frameworks.

C) It automates the entire testing workflow.

D) It generates compliance certificates for test cases.

Answer: B

Explanation: Copilot suggests boilerplate testing code for various frameworks, reducing the time spent on repetitive tasks and improving developer productivity.

351. How does GitHub Copilot help developers stay consistent with project-specific terminologies?

A) By automating pull request approvals.

B) By suggesting code and comments that align with project-specific terminologies.

C) By disabling conflicting terminologies across files.

D) By generating compliance reports for language consistency.

Answer: B

Explanation: Copilot helps developers stay consistent by suggesting code and comments that align with project-specific terminologies, ensuring uniformity.

352. Which GitHub Copilot Labs feature can help developers refactor large codebases?

A) Code Transformation

B) Security Auditing

C) Feedback Mechanism

D) Role-Based Licensing

Answer: A

Explanation: The Code Transformation feature in GitHub Copilot Labs helps developers refactor large codebases by suggesting optimized and updated code structures.

353. How does Copilot assist in reducing errors during code integration?

A) By automating repository duplication.

B) By suggesting fixes for integration-related issues based on context.

C) By disabling conflicting code snippets.

D) By generating compliance certificates for integrations.

Answer: B

Explanation: Copilot suggests fixes for integration-related issues, helping developers reduce errors and maintain smooth code integration processes.

354. What is a unique benefit of using GitHub Copilot for cross-platform applications?

A) It automates platform-specific testing workflows.

B) It provides context-aware suggestions tailored to each platform.

C) It disables unsupported platform features.

D) It generates compliance reports for multi-platform projects.

Answer: B

Explanation: Copilot provides context-aware suggestions tailored to each platform, simplifying development for cross-platform applications.

355. Which GitHub Copilot feature is most effective for brainstorming algorithm implementations?

A) Pull Request Automation

B) Context-Aware Suggestions

C) Role-Based Licensing

D) Repository Duplication Tools

Answer: B

Explanation: Context-aware suggestions enable developers to brainstorm algorithm implementations by providing relevant and efficient code snippets.

356. How does GitHub Copilot support project scalability?

A) By automating code reviews for scale.

B) By providing modular and reusable code suggestions.

C) By disabling less critical modules automatically.

D) By generating compliance certifications for large projects.

Answer: B

Explanation: Copilot supports project scalability by suggesting modular and reusable code, enabling teams to adapt and grow their projects efficiently.

357. What is a key feature of GitHub Copilot for simplifying

collaborative workflows?

A) Automated Workflow Integration

B) Consistent Suggestions for Shared Codebases

C) Automated Repository Duplication

D) Security Auditing for Collaborative Workflows

Answer: B

Explanation: Copilot simplifies collaborative workflows by providing consistent suggestions for shared codebases, ensuring alignment across teams.

358. How can developers use GitHub Copilot to improve code readability?

A) By automating pull requests.

B) By receiving suggestions that follow clean coding principles.

C) By disabling conflicting code styles.

D) By generating compliance reports for readability.

Answer: B

Explanation: Copilot improves code readability by providing suggestions that follow clean coding principles and best practices.

Domain 7: Security and Compliance

359. How can GitHub Copilot help ensure secure code practices?

A) By automating repository creation.

B) By suggesting best practices for secure coding during development.

C) By disabling manual coding workflows.

D) By automatically encrypting all repositories.

Answer: B

Explanation: GitHub Copilot helps ensure secure code practices by suggesting best practices for secure coding during development, reducing vulnerabilities.

360. What is the best way to prevent Copilot from exposing sensitive information?

A) Disable Copilot for private repositories.

B) Avoid including sensitive data, such as API keys, in your codebase.

C) Share sensitive data in comments for better suggestions.

D) Use Copilot only in public repositories.

Answer: B

Explanation: Avoid including sensitive data, such as API keys or credentials, in your codebase to prevent Copilot from inadvertently exposing it.

361. How does GitHub Copilot support compliance in regulated industries?

A) By replacing manual compliance reviews.

B) By adhering to privacy regulations like GDPR, HIPAA, and ISO 27001.

C) By automating repository duplication.

D) By disabling pull requests from unverified contributors.

Answer: B

Explanation: GitHub Copilot supports compliance in regulated industries by adhering to privacy regulations like GDPR, HIPAA, and ISO 27001.

362. What role do audit logs play in compliance monitoring?

A) They automate pull request approvals.

B) They track user activities and provide visibility for compliance audits.

C) They disable unused repositories automatically.

D) They generate compliance certificates.

Answer: B

Explanation: Audit logs track user activities and provide visibility for compliance audits, helping organizations maintain accountability.

363. How can developers ensure secure code when using Copilot?

A) Review all Copilot suggestions for security vulnerabilities before implementation.

B) Disable Copilot for sensitive projects.

C) Automate security checks within Copilot.

D) Share sensitive information for better suggestions.

Answer: A

Explanation: Developers should review all Copilot suggestions for security vulnerabilities before implementing them to ensure secure code.

364. What is a key compliance feature of GitHub Copilot Business?

A) Unlimited repository creation.

B) Audit logs for tracking activities and ensuring compliance.

C) Automated pull request approvals.

D) Role-based licensing.

Answer: B

Explanation: Audit logs track activities and ensure compliance, making them a key feature for organizations using GitHub Copilot Business.

365. Which of the following is an example of sensitive information that should not be included in codebases?

A) Variable names

B) API keys and credentials

C) Function definitions

D) Inline comments

Answer: B

Explanation: Sensitive information, like API keys and credentials, should never be included in codebases as they can be exposed inadvertently.

366. How does GitHub Copilot handle proprietary code in private repositories?

A) It disables suggestions for private repositories.

B) It does not retain or share proprietary code, ensuring data privacy.

C) It stores proprietary code for generating better suggestions.

D) It automatically encrypts all proprietary code.

Answer: B

Explanation: GitHub Copilot does not retain or share proprietary code from private repositories, ensuring data privacy and security.

367. What is the purpose of role-based access controls in GitHub Copilot Business?

A) To automate repository creation.

B) To restrict access to resources based on user roles, ensuring secure collaboration.

C) To disable unused licenses.

D) To replace manual pull request reviews.

Answer: B

Explanation: Role-based access controls restrict access to resources based on user roles, ensuring secure collaboration across teams.

368. Which compliance standard is directly supported by GitHub Copilot for healthcare organizations?

A) PCI DSS

B) HIPAA

C) SOX

D) ISO 9001

Answer: B

Explanation: GitHub Copilot supports HIPAA compliance, making it suitable for healthcare organizations that handle sensitive patient data.

369. How can developers avoid Copilot suggestions that might violate copyright laws?

A) Use Copilot only for private projects.

B) Validate the originality of Copilot-generated code and ensure proper attribution.

C) Share open-source code in all repositories.

D) Disable Copilot for non-critical tasks.

Answer: B

Explanation: Developers should validate the originality of Copilot-generated code and ensure proper attribution to avoid copyright violations.

370. What is a potential risk of using Copilot in unregulated industries?

A) Lack of repository duplication features.

B) Exposure to biased or incomplete code suggestions.

C) Inability to generate boilerplate code.

D) Reduced coding speed.

Answer: B

Explanation: A potential risk of using Copilot in unregulated industries is exposure to biased or incomplete code suggestions, which may lead to vulnerabilities.

371. What is the role of encryption in GitHub Copilot Business?

A) To generate compliance reports.

B) To ensure secure communication and protect sensitive data.

C) To automate pull request approvals.

D) To disable private repositories.

Answer: B

Explanation: Encryption ensures secure communication and protects sensitive data, making it a critical feature of GitHub Copilot Business.

372. How does GitHub Copilot ensure compliance with GDPR?

A) By automating compliance audits.

B) By not storing user code and adhering to strict data protection measures.

C) By disabling private repositories.

D) By generating compliance certificates.

Answer: B

Explanation: GitHub Copilot ensures compliance with GDPR by adhering to strict data protection measures and not storing user code.

373. What is the purpose of audit logs in regulated industries?

A) To disable unused repositories.

B) To provide detailed records for compliance audits.

C) To automate repository creation.

D) To replace manual coding workflows.

Answer: B

Explanation: Audit logs provide detailed records of user activities, making them essential for compliance audits in regulated industries.

374. Which of the following is a security best practice when using GitHub Copilot?

A) Share sensitive data for better suggestions.

B) Validate all suggestions for potential vulnerabilities.

C) Use Copilot only in public repositories.

D) Automate testing workflows.

Answer: B

Explanation: Validating all suggestions for potential vulnerabilities is a security best practice when using GitHub Copilot.

375. How does centralized management in GitHub Copilot Business benefit security?

A) By automating pull request approvals.

B) By allowing administrators to control access and monitor activities.

C) By generating compliance certificates.

D) By disabling unused repositories automatically.

Answer: B

Explanation: Centralized management allows administrators to control access and monitor activities, enhancing security in GitHub Copilot Business.

376. What is the purpose of compliance tools in GitHub Copilot Business?

A) To automate repository backups.

B) To ensure adherence to industry standards and regulations.

C) To replace manual coding workflows.

D) To disable non-critical pull requests.

Answer: B

Explanation: Compliance tools ensure adherence to industry standards and regulations, making GitHub Copilot Business suitable for regulated industries.

377. How can developers ensure Copilot suggestions are free from potential security risks?

A) Automate all testing workflows.

B) Conduct thorough reviews and integrate static code analysis tools.

C) Use Copilot only for non-critical projects.

D) Disable Copilot for private repositories.

Answer: B

Explanation: Developers can ensure Copilot suggestions are secure by conducting thorough reviews and integrating static code analysis tools.

378. Which GitHub Copilot feature ensures sensitive data is not retained?

A) Automated Repository Duplication

B) Privacy-First Data Handling

C) Pull Request Automation

D) Multi-Language Support

Answer: B

Explanation: GitHub Copilot uses privacy-first data handling to ensure sensitive data is not retained or shared, protecting user privacy.

379. Which of the following is a secure practice when handling proprietary code in GitHub Copilot?

A) Sharing proprietary code in public repositories.

B) Reviewing all Copilot suggestions to ensure they align with project requirements.

C) Allowing unrestricted access to proprietary repositories.

D) Using Copilot only in experimental projects.

Answer: B

Explanation: Reviewing Copilot suggestions ensures they align with project requirements and do not inadvertently expose proprietary code.

380. What is the primary benefit of using audit logs in GitHub Copilot Business?

A) They automate pull request approvals.

B) They provide a detailed history of user actions for compliance and security tracking.

C) They disable unused repositories.

D) They generate secure backups of all repositories.

Answer: B

Explanation: Audit logs provide a detailed history of user actions, aiding in compliance and security tracking within an organization.

381. How does GitHub Copilot help developers avoid introducing vulnerabilities in their code?

A) By encrypting all files in the repository.

B) By suggesting secure coding practices based on context.

C) By disabling unused code snippets.

D) By automating manual security audits.

Answer: B

Explanation: GitHub Copilot suggests secure coding practices based on context, helping developers avoid introducing vulnerabilities.

382. Why is it important to validate Copilot-generated code for compliance in regulated industries?

A) To automate repository creation.

B) To ensure it meets industry-specific legal and security standards.

C) To disable private repository features.

D) To replace manual coding workflows.

Answer: B

Explanation: Validating Copilot-generated code ensures it meets industry-specific legal and security standards, avoiding compliance risks.

383. What is the best practice for handling sensitive information in a shared repository?

A) Encrypt sensitive information directly in the codebase.

B) Store sensitive information securely outside the repository.

C) Share sensitive information in comments for clarity.

D) Disable access to private repositories.

Answer: B

Explanation: Sensitive information should be stored securely outside the repository to prevent unauthorized access or accidental exposure.

384. How does GitHub Copilot help maintain security in multi-developer teams?

A) By automating repository duplication.

B) By providing role-based access controls and secure coding suggestions.

C) By disabling conflicting pull requests.

D) By generating compliance certificates for each developer.

Answer: B

Explanation: Role-based access controls and secure coding suggestions help maintain security in multi-developer teams using GitHub Copilot.

385. Which compliance framework is supported by GitHub Copilot for financial institutions?

A) ISO 14001

B) PCI DSS

C) GDPR

D) HIPAA

Answer: B

Explanation: GitHub Copilot supports compliance frameworks like PCI DSS, which are essential for financial institutions handling payment data.

386. What is the potential risk of using Copilot in open-source projects?

A) Reduced collaboration efficiency.

B) Exposure to licensing or copyright issues in generated code.

C) Inability to handle large codebases.

D) Slower suggestion speeds.

Answer: B

Explanation: Using Copilot in open-source projects may expose teams to licensing or copyright issues if the generated code resembles proprietary content.

387. How does GitHub Copilot Business ensure data privacy in cloud-hosted environments?

A) By storing all data locally on user machines.

B) By encrypting communications and ensuring compliance with privacy regulations.

C) By disabling repository access for external collaborators.

D) By automating privacy audits.

Answer: B

Explanation: GitHub Copilot Business ensures data privacy in cloud-hosted environments by encrypting communications and adhering to privacy regulations.

388. Which GitHub Copilot feature can help organizations track

compliance violations?

A) Pull Request Automation

B) Audit Logs

C) Role-Based Licensing

D) Automated Code Refactoring

Answer: B

Explanation: Audit logs help organizations track compliance violations by providing detailed records of user activities.

389. Why is it important to monitor Copilot usage in regulated industries?

A) To automate repository creation.

B) To ensure compliance with industry standards and avoid data breaches.

C) To disable unused repositories.

D) To simplify manual workflows.

Answer: B

Explanation: Monitoring Copilot usage ensures compliance with industry standards and helps prevent data breaches in regulated industries.

390. How can GitHub Copilot suggestions be optimized for secure coding?

A) By enabling auto-approval of pull requests.

B) By integrating Copilot with static code analysis tools for validation.

C) By storing sensitive data in the codebase.

D) By disabling suggestions for private repositories.

Answer: B

Explanation: Integrating Copilot with static code analysis tools allows developers to validate suggestions for secure coding practices.

391. Which feature of GitHub Copilot Business enhances security in collaborative environments?

A) Automated Testing Tools

B) Role-Based Access Controls

C) Unlimited Public Repositories

D) Multi-Factor Authentication

Answer: B

Explanation: Role-based access controls enhance security in collaborative environments by restricting access based on user roles.

392. How does GitHub Copilot handle sensitive data in private repositories?

A) By encrypting all repository content.

B) By not storing or retaining sensitive data from private repositories.

C) By generating compliance certificates for sensitive data.

D) By disabling access to sensitive files.

Answer: B

Explanation: GitHub Copilot does not store or retain sensitive data from private repositories, maintaining data privacy and security.

393. What is the role of encryption in GitHub Copilot Business?

A) To automate testing workflows.

B) To secure communications and protect sensitive information.

C) To disable unused repositories.

D) To replace manual security audits.

Answer: B

Explanation: Encryption secures communications and protects sensitive information, making it a critical component of GitHub Copilot Business.

394. Which of the following is a security risk when using Copilot without validation?

A) Reduced development speed.

B) Introduction of code with potential vulnerabilities.

C) Slower repository creation.

D) Lack of access to public repositories.

Answer: B

Explanation: Using Copilot without validation may introduce code with potential vulnerabilities, posing a security risk to the project.

395. How does GitHub Copilot align with GDPR compliance?

A) By automating compliance audits.

B) By adhering to strict data protection policies and not storing user code.

C) By disabling access to private repositories.

D) By generating compliance certificates for European users.

Answer: B

Explanation: GitHub Copilot aligns with GDPR compliance by adhering to strict data protection policies and not storing user code.

396. What is a key step to securely using Copilot in financial applications?

A) Automate repository duplication.

B) Validate all code suggestions for compliance with PCI DSS.

C) Disable Copilot for private repositories.

D) Store financial data directly in the codebase.

Answer: B

Explanation: Validating all code suggestions ensures compliance with PCI DSS, making Copilot suitable for financial applications.

398. How can developers ensure that Copilot-generated code does not violate intellectual property rights?

A) By automating testing workflows.

B) By validating the originality of suggestions and avoiding direct use of copyrighted code.

C) By disabling Copilot for experimental projects.

D) By sharing all generated code publicly.

Answer: B

Explanation: Developers should validate the originality of Copilot's suggestions and avoid using copyrighted code directly to prevent intellectual property violations.

399. Which security feature in GitHub Copilot Business prevents unauthorized access?

A) Role-Based Access Controls

B) Automated Pull Request Approvals

C) Repository Duplication Tools

D) Multi-Language Support

Answer: A

Explanation: Role-based access controls prevent unauthorized access by restricting resources based on user roles.

400. What is the primary advantage of using GitHub Copilot for secure code reviews?

A) It automates all review tasks.

B) It identifies common security vulnerabilities in real-time suggestions.

C) It disables pull requests with potential vulnerabilities.

D) It replaces manual code reviews entirely.

Answer: B

Explanation: GitHub Copilot helps identify common security vulnerabilities through real-time suggestions, improving code security during reviews.

401. How can organizations prevent unauthorized access to repositories when using GitHub Copilot?

A) By automating repository duplication.

B) By enabling multi-factor authentication (MFA) for all users.

C) By disabling Copilot in private repositories.

D) By allowing guest access for external contributors.

Answer: B

Explanation: Enabling multi-factor authentication (MFA) ensures only authorized users can access repositories, enhancing security.

402. Which GitHub Copilot practice ensures compliance with intellectual property laws?

A) Disabling Copilot for shared projects.

B) Validating that Copilot suggestions do not resemble copyrighted code.

C) Automating compliance reporting workflows.

D) Using Copilot only in public repositories.

Answer: B

Explanation: Validating Copilot suggestions ensures they do not resemble copyrighted code, maintaining compliance with intellectual property laws.

403. What is the benefit of using GitHub Copilot in projects with strict regulatory requirements?

A) It automates all compliance checks.

B) It suggests code that adheres to industry standards and best practices.

C) It disables irrelevant repositories automatically.

D) It generates compliance reports for every commit.

Answer: B

Explanation: GitHub Copilot suggests code that adheres to industry standards and best practices, making it suitable for projects with strict regulatory requirements.

404. How does GitHub Copilot protect sensitive information during code generation?

A) By encrypting generated code snippets.

B) By not storing or retaining any user data from private repositories.

C) By disabling suggestions for sensitive projects.

D) By generating compliance reports for sensitive files.

Answer: B

Explanation: GitHub Copilot protects sensitive information by not storing or retaining user data from private repositories, ensuring privacy.

405. What is a common security risk when using Copilot in collaborative projects?

A) Lack of role-based access controls.

B) Exposure to insecure or biased code suggestions.

C) Inability to generate secure boilerplate code.

D) Reduced visibility into repository activity.

Answer: B

Explanation: Using Copilot without validation may expose teams to insecure or biased code suggestions, posing a security risk.

406. How can audit logs improve security in GitHub Copilot Business?

A) By automating repository creation.

B) By providing visibility into user actions and accessing logs for suspicious activity.

C) By disabling unverified pull requests.

D) By generating compliance reports for every repository.

Answer: B

Explanation: Audit logs provide visibility into user actions, allowing administrators to monitor suspicious activity and improve security.

407. Which compliance regulation is critical for organizations handling financial transactions and using GitHub Copilot?

A) HIPAA

B) PCI DSS

C) GDPR

D) ISO 14001

Answer: B

Explanation: PCI DSS is critical for organizations handling financial transactions, ensuring secure handling of payment data.

408. What is the primary purpose of role-based access controls in GitHub Copilot Business?

A) To automate pull request reviews.

B) To restrict access to sensitive resources based on user roles.

C) To enable guest access for external collaborators.

D) To generate compliance certificates.

Answer: B

Explanation: Role-based access controls restrict access to sensitive resources based on user roles, enhancing security in collaborative environments.

409. Which GitHub Copilot feature helps developers identify and fix security vulnerabilities?

A) Multi-language support.

B) Context-aware coding suggestions for security.

C) Automated repository duplication.

D) Real-time compliance certificates.

Answer: B

Explanation: Context-aware coding suggestions help developers identify and fix security vulnerabilities during development.

410. How does GitHub Copilot ensure compliance in industries with strict data privacy laws?

A) By automating compliance audits.

B) By encrypting communications and not storing user code.

C) By disabling private repositories.

D) By generating compliance reports for all pull requests.

Answer: B

Explanation: GitHub Copilot encrypts communications and does not store user code, ensuring compliance with data privacy laws like GDPR.

411. What is a potential issue to consider when using Copilot-generated code in regulated industries?

A) It may disable role-based access controls.

B) It may generate code that does not meet specific regulatory requirements.

C) It cannot handle multi-language projects.

D) It may reduce collaboration speed.

Answer: B

Explanation: Copilot-generated code may not meet specific regulatory requirements, making validation essential in regulated industries.

412. Which GitHub Copilot feature supports secure collaboration in remote teams?

A) Automated repository backups.

B) Role-based access controls combined with encrypted communications.

C) Unlimited public repositories.

D) Real-time compliance reporting.

Answer: B

Explanation: Role-based access controls and encrypted communications ensure secure collaboration in remote teams using GitHub Copilot.

413. Why is it important to validate Copilot-generated code for proprietary projects?

A) To automate testing workflows.

B) To ensure it aligns with internal standards and does not expose proprietary logic.

C) To disable unused repositories.

D) To enable faster pull request approvals.

Answer: B

Explanation: Validating Copilot-generated code ensures it aligns with internal standards and does not expose proprietary logic or sensitive information.

414. How can developers improve the security of Copilot suggestions in sensitive applications?

A) By sharing sensitive data with Copilot for better suggestions.

B) By validating and testing all suggestions before implementation.

C) By disabling Copilot for sensitive projects.

D) By automating security audits for all suggestions.

Answer: B

Developers should validate and test all suggestions before implementation to improve the security of Copilot-generated code in sensitive applications.

415. What is the role of GitHub Copilot in ensuring compliance with ISO 27001?

A) It automates compliance reporting workflows.

B) It provides secure coding suggestions and maintains data privacy.

C) It disables irrelevant repositories automatically.

D) It generates encrypted reports for ISO audits.

Answer: B

Explanation: GitHub Copilot supports ISO 27001 compliance by providing secure coding suggestions and maintaining data privacy.

416. Which GitHub Copilot practice can help prevent data leaks in collaborative environments?

A) Automating repository duplication.

B) Using role-based access controls and avoiding sensitive data in the codebase.

C) Sharing sensitive data securely within the repository.

D) Disabling pull requests for external contributors.

Answer: B

Explanation: Using role-based access controls and avoiding sensitive data in the codebase helps prevent data leaks in collaborative environments.

417. What is a critical step when using Copilot for government or defense-related projects?

A) Automate compliance reviews for pull requests.

B) Validate that all code complies with applicable legal and regulatory standards.

C) Share sensitive information within private repositories.

D) Disable access to unused repositories.

Answer: B

Explanation: Validating that all code complies with applicable legal and regulatory standards is critical when using Copilot for government or defense-related projects.

418. How does GitHub Copilot protect against unauthorized access to sensitive repositories?

A) By automating repository creation.

B) By integrating role-based access controls and multi-factor authentication.

C) By disabling access for remote collaborators.

D) By encrypting all repository backups.

Answer: B

Explanation: GitHub Copilot protects against unauthorized access by integrating role-based access controls and multi-factor authentication.

419. What is the security advantage of validating Copilot suggestions in CI/CD pipelines?

A) It automates repository duplication for faster deployment.

B) It ensures Copilot-generated code meets security and compliance requirements before deployment.

C) It disables unused repositories to improve performance.

D) It generates compliance certificates for all pipeline stages.

Answer: B

Explanation: Validating Copilot suggestions in CI/CD pipelines ensures the code meets security and compliance requirements before deployment.

Domain 8: Practical Applications and Troubleshooting

420. Which GitHub Copilot feature is most useful for debugging functional programming code?

A) Automated testing workflows.

B) Context-aware suggestions for recursive or pure functions.

C) Repository duplication tools.

D) Multi-language code generation.

Answer: B

Explanation: Copilot's context-aware suggestions are especially helpful in debugging functional programming code by offering solutions tailored to recursive or pure functions.

421. How can Copilot assist in writing code using object-oriented programming (OOP) principles?

A) By disabling manual coding workflows.

B) By suggesting class definitions, methods, and inheritance structures.

C) By automating repository creation for object-oriented projects.

D) By generating compliance certificates for OOP standards.

Answer: B

Explanation: Copilot assists in OOP by suggesting class definitions, methods, and inheritance structures, helping developers follow best practices.

422. What is a practical approach to troubleshooting when Copilot

provides irrelevant suggestions?

A) Disable Copilot for complex projects.

B) Provide more detailed comments or context in your code.

C) Automate suggestion filtering workflows.

D) Use Copilot only for standalone scripts.

Answer: B

Explanation: Providing more detailed comments or context helps Copilot generate more relevant and accurate suggestions.

423. How can Copilot improve efficiency in debugging DevOps pipeline scripts?

A) By automating pipeline execution.

B) By suggesting fixes for syntax errors and broken configurations.

C) By disabling unused scripts in the pipeline.

D) By generating compliance certificates for pipeline security.

Answer: B

Explanation: Copilot improves efficiency in debugging DevOps pipeline scripts by suggesting fixes for syntax errors and broken configurations.

424. What is a key consideration when using Copilot to write functional programming code?

A) Avoid using recursion entirely.

B) Ensure that generated code adheres to immutability and pure function principles.

C) Automate testing for all suggestions.

D) Disable Copilot for multi-step functions.

Answer: B

Explanation: In functional programming, it is important to ensure that Copilot-generated code adheres to immutability and pure function principles.

425. Which Copilot feature is most useful for identifying performance bottlenecks in code?

A) Suggestion Feedback

B) Context-Aware Profiling Suggestions

C) Automated Pull Request Approvals

D) Repository Duplication Tools

Answer: B

Explanation: Context-aware profiling suggestions help developers identify performance bottlenecks in their code.

426. What is the best method to integrate Copilot into a CI/CD workflow?

A) Automate all build stages with Copilot.

B) Use Copilot to generate pipeline scripts and validate them with automated tests.

C) Disable Copilot for CI/CD workflows.

D) Rely solely on Copilot for deployment.

Answer: B

Explanation: Use Copilot to generate pipeline scripts and validate them with automated tests to ensure correctness in CI/CD workflows.

427. How can Copilot assist in debugging multi-threaded applications?

A) By disabling multi-threading features.

B) By suggesting thread-safe code and identifying potential race conditions.

C) By automating thread management workflows.

D) By replacing manual debugging tools.

Answer: B

Explanation: Copilot assists in debugging multi-threaded applications by suggesting thread-safe code and identifying potential race conditions.

428. What is the practical use of Copilot in functional programming for performance optimization?

A) Automating recursive function calls.

B) Suggesting optimized higher-order functions and avoiding side effects.

C) Disabling complex functional constructs.

D) Generating compliance reports for functional code.

Answer: B

Explanation: Copilot can suggest optimized higher-order functions and help avoid side effects, improving performance in functional programming.

429. How can Copilot help troubleshoot issues in event-driven programming?

A) By automating event logging.

B) By suggesting fixes for event handler logic and debugging asynchronous flows.

C) By disabling event-driven workflows.

D) By generating compliance certificates for event handlers.

Answer: B

Explanation: Copilot suggests fixes for event handler logic and helps debug asynchronous flows, aiding in troubleshooting event-driven programming.

430. What is a key advantage of using Copilot in writing declarative programming code?

A) It automates repository duplication.

B) It suggests concise, goal-oriented code that follows declarative principles.

C) It disables imperative constructs in the codebase.

D) It generates compliance reports for declarative syntax.

Answer: B

Explanation: Copilot suggests concise, goal-oriented code that aligns with declarative programming principles, improving readability and maintainability.

431. What is the best way to debug Copilot-suggested code that causes errors in production?

A) Automate testing for all suggestions before deployment.

B) Disable Copilot in production environments.

C) Replace generated code with manual implementations.

D) Use Copilot only for testing purposes.

Answer: A

Explanation: Automating tests for Copilot-suggested code ensures that errors are caught before deployment to production.

432. How can Copilot enhance collaboration in DevOps workflows?

A) By automating deployment approvals.

B) By providing consistent suggestions for pipeline scripts, ensuring team alignment.

C) By disabling unused stages in the pipeline.

D) By generating compliance certificates for all workflows.

Answer: B

Explanation: Copilot provides consistent suggestions for pipeline scripts, ensuring that team members follow the same standards and workflows.

433. What is a practical application of Copilot in reactive programming?

A) Automating observable subscriptions.

B) Suggesting efficient ways to handle streams and reactive data flows.

C) Disabling reactive constructs in the codebase.

D) Generating compliance reports for reactive systems.

Answer: B

Explanation: Copilot suggests efficient ways to handle streams and reactive data flows, making it a valuable tool for reactive programming.

434. How does Copilot assist in identifying code smells in object-oriented programming?

A) By automating code refactoring.

B) By suggesting improvements to class design and method structures.

C) By disabling complex inheritance hierarchies.

D) By replacing manual debugging tools.

Answer: B

Explanation: Copilot suggests improvements to class design and method structures, helping developers identify and address code smells in OOP.

435. What is the role of Copilot in debugging functional code with higher-order functions?

A) It disables higher-order constructs.

B) It suggests optimized implementations for higher-order functions.

C) It automates debugging for all functional constructs.

D) It replaces manual testing entirely.

Answer: B

Explanation: Copilot suggests optimized implementations for higher-order functions, improving the debugging process in functional programming.

436. How does Copilot simplify writing test cases for DevOps pipelines?

A) By automating pipeline execution.

B) By generating boilerplate test cases based on pipeline logic.

C) By disabling unused pipeline stages.

D) By replacing manual testing with automated workflows.

Answer: B

Explanation: Copilot generates boilerplate test cases based on pipeline logic, simplifying the process of writing tests for DevOps workflows.

437. How can Copilot assist in debugging race conditions in concurrent programming?

A) By automating thread management.

B) By suggesting thread-safe solutions and identifying shared resource conflicts.

C) By disabling multi-threading features in the codebase.

D) By generating compliance certificates for concurrent applications.

Answer: B

Explanation: Copilot suggests thread-safe solutions and identifies shared resource conflicts, helping developers debug race conditions in concurrent programming.

438. What is a key practical use of Copilot for troubleshooting CI/CD pipelines?

A) Automating deployment approvals.

B) Suggesting fixes for broken stages and misconfigured workflows.

C) Disabling unused pipeline stages automatically.

D) Generating compliance reports for all workflows.

Answer: B

Explanation: Copilot suggests fixes for broken stages and misconfigured workflows, making it a valuable tool for troubleshooting CI/CD pipelines.

439. How can Copilot be used to troubleshoot errors in declarative programming frameworks?

A) By automating framework-specific testing.

B) By suggesting concise, goal-oriented fixes for syntax or logic errors.

C) By disabling declarative constructs in the codebase.

D) By generating compliance certificates for framework usage.

Answer: B

Explanation: Copilot suggests concise, goal-oriented fixes for syntax or logic errors in declarative programming frameworks.

440. How can Copilot assist in troubleshooting memory leaks in object-oriented programming?

A) By automating garbage collection.

B) By suggesting best practices for object lifecycle management and memory allocation.

C) By disabling unused class instances.

D) By generating compliance certificates for memory management.

Answer: B

Explanation: Copilot can suggest best practices for managing object lifecycles, such as proper use of destructors, avoiding circular references, and managing dynamic memory allocation. These suggestions help developers avoid memory leaks.

441. What is a practical use of Copilot in debugging serverless applications?

A) Automating function deployment to the cloud.

B) Providing suggestions to optimize cold start times and fix misconfigured triggers.

C) Disabling unused serverless functions.

D) Replacing manual testing with AI-generated workflows.

Answer: B

Explanation: Copilot can help identify and resolve issues like slow cold start times, misconfigured event triggers, or inefficient function invocations, which are common challenges in serverless computing.

442. How can Copilot assist in writing unit tests for functional programming?

A) By automating recursive function calls.

B) By generating test cases for pure functions based on input-output mappings.

C) By disabling side effects in all functions.

D) By replacing unit tests with integration tests.

Answer: B

Explanation: Functional programming relies heavily on pure functions. Copilot can generate unit test cases that validate the expected output for a given input, ensuring correctness without side effects.

443. What is the best way to troubleshoot Copilot suggestions that conflict with existing coding standards?

A) Disable Copilot for the affected project.

B) Customize the comments and context to guide Copilot toward the desired standard.

C) Use Copilot only for specific languages.

D) Automate the enforcement of coding standards.

Answer: B

Explanation: By providing clearer comments and context, developers can guide Copilot to generate suggestions that align with the project's coding standards, reducing conflicts.

444. How can Copilot help optimize database queries in DevOps workflows?

A) By automating schema migrations.

B) By suggesting optimized SQL queries based on the database schema.

C) By disabling complex joins in the queries.

D) By generating compliance reports for database operations.

Answer: B

Explanation: Copilot can analyze query patterns and suggest optimizations like indexing, avoiding unnecessary joins, or reordering clauses to improve efficiency and reduce execution time.

445. What is a common troubleshooting step when Copilot fails to provide relevant suggestions in a multi-language project?

A) Disable Copilot for less-used languages.

B) Ensure the file and project have sufficient context and comments for Copilot to analyze.

C) Automate language-specific testing workflows.

D) Use Copilot only for the primary language of the project.

Answer: B

Explanation: Copilot relies on context to generate relevant suggestions. If sufficient comments or metadata are missing, it may fail to provide accurate recommendations, especially in multi-language projects.

446. How can Copilot assist in debugging asynchronous code in JavaScript?

A) By replacing promises with synchronous functions.

B) By suggesting better error-handling mechanisms and identifying unhandled promises.

C) By disabling async/await constructs.

D) By automating callback execution.

Answer: B

Explanation: Copilot can suggest improved error-handling mechanisms for promises and async/await constructs, ensuring unhandled promises and errors are properly addressed in the code.

447. What is a practical application of Copilot in debugging race

conditions in distributed systems?

A) Automating all data synchronization tasks.

B) Suggesting thread-safe mechanisms for shared resources and locks.

C) Disabling parallel execution.

D) Replacing distributed systems with centralized ones.

Answer: B

Explanation: Copilot can identify potential race conditions and suggest thread-safe mechanisms, such as locks, semaphores, or atomic operations, to ensure proper synchronization in distributed systems.

448. How does Copilot help troubleshoot misconfigured CI/CD pipeline stages?

A) By disabling the affected stages.

B) By suggesting fixes for misconfigured steps, such as invalid paths or missing dependencies.

C) By automating the entire CI/CD workflow.

D) By generating compliance reports for pipeline configurations.

Answer: B

Explanation: Copilot analyzes pipeline scripts and suggests fixes for common misconfigurations, such as incorrect file paths, missing dependencies, or environment variable issues.

449. What is a recommended practice when Copilot suggests inefficient algorithms?

A) Disable Copilot for algorithm-heavy projects.

B) Refine the comments to specify the desired algorithm type or complexity constraints.

C) Automate the generation of all algorithms.

D) Use Copilot suggestions without validation.

Answer: B

Explanation: Providing detailed comments about the desired algorithm type, complexity, or constraints helps Copilot generate more efficient and appropriate suggestions.

450. How can Copilot assist in writing parallel processing code?

A) By disabling multi-threading features.

B) By suggesting efficient task distribution and thread-pooling mechanisms.

C) By automating thread creation workflows.

D) By generating compliance certificates for parallel code.

Answer: B

Explanation: Copilot can suggest efficient ways to distribute tasks across threads and implement thread-pooling mechanisms, improving the performance of parallel processing code.

451. How does Copilot help manage large-scale microservices in DevOps pipelines?

A) By automating service deployment.

B) By generating service-specific configurations and health-check scripts.

C) By disabling unused microservices.

D) By replacing manual service orchestration.

Answer: B

Explanation: Copilot generates configurations and health-check scripts tailored to each microservice, simplifying management in large-scale DevOps pipelines.

452. What is a practical use of Copilot in debugging dependency injection issues in object-oriented programming?

A) Automating dependency injection frameworks.

B) Suggesting correct configurations and resolving circular dependencies.

C) Disabling unused dependencies.

D) Replacing dependency injection with static references.

Answer: B

Explanation: Copilot helps resolve dependency injection issues by suggesting correct configurations and identifying circular dependencies or misconfigurations.

453. How can Copilot streamline debugging in reactive programming frameworks?

A) By automating observable subscriptions.

B) By suggesting efficient ways to handle reactive streams and resolve backpressure problems.

C) By disabling reactive constructs in the codebase.

D) By generating compliance reports for reactive systems.

Answer: B

Explanation: Copilot offers suggestions for handling reactive streams and resolving backpressure problems, improving debugging in reactive programming frameworks.

454. What is a recommended approach when Copilot suggestions fail to align with functional programming principles?

A) Disable Copilot for functional programming projects.

B) Include comments emphasizing immutability and statelessness.

C) Automate all functional constructs.

D) Use Copilot only for imperative programming.

Answer: B

Explanation: Including comments about immutability and statelessness guides Copilot to generate suggestions that align with functional programming principles.

455. How can Copilot assist in troubleshooting misaligned APIs in DevOps workflows?

A) By automating API versioning.

B) By suggesting fixes for API request formats and resolving mismatched endpoints.

C) By disabling outdated APIs.

D) By generating compliance certificates for API usage.

Answer: B

Explanation: Copilot helps resolve API issues by suggesting fixes for request formats, headers, and mismatched endpoints, ensuring smooth integration in workflows.

456. What is a key advantage of using Copilot for debugging recursive functions?

A) Automating recursive iterations.

B) Suggesting base cases and termination conditions to avoid infinite recursion.

C) Disabling recursion in favor of iterative solutions.

D) Replacing recursion with functional constructs.

Answer: B

Explanation: Copilot suggests appropriate base cases and termination conditions, preventing infinite recursion and improving reliability.

457. How can Copilot enhance logging practices in DevOps pipelines?

A) By automating log ingestion workflows.

B) By suggesting meaningful log messages and structured logging formats.

C) By disabling verbose logging in production.

D) By generating compliance reports for log storage.

Answer: B

Explanation: Copilot can suggest meaningful log messages and structured logging formats, making logs more useful for debugging and monitoring in DevOps pipelines.

458. How does Copilot help in debugging state management issues in object-oriented programming?

A) Automating state synchronization.

B) Suggesting solutions for state inconsistencies and proper encapsulation.

C) Disabling stateful objects in the codebase.

D) Replacing stateful designs with stateless ones.

Answer: B

Explanation: Copilot suggests solutions for managing state inconsistencies and encapsulation, ensuring proper state management in object-oriented programming.

459. What is a practical approach when Copilot suggests overly complex solutions for simple problems?

A) Disable Copilot for small projects.

B) Refine comments to emphasize simplicity and avoid over-engineering.

C) Use Copilot only for large-scale applications.

D) Automate complexity reduction workflows.

Answer: B

Explanation: Providing comments that emphasize simplicity helps Copilot generate more straightforward and appropriate solutions for simple problems.

460. How can Copilot assist in debugging a circular dependency issue in modular programming?

A) By disabling dependency imports in affected modules.

B) By suggesting alternative design patterns to break the dependency cycle.

C) By automating dependency resolution in all modules.

D) By replacing modular design with monolithic architecture.

Answer: B

Explanation: Circular dependencies can cause runtime issues or infinite loops in modular programming. Copilot can suggest alternative design patterns, such as dependency injection or moving shared logic to a separate module, to resolve the issue.

461. What is a practical troubleshooting step if Copilot suggests unsafe code practices for handling user input?

A) Disable Copilot for input validation routines.

B) Add comments emphasizing the need for secure input validation.

C) Automate testing for all input-handling code.

D) Replace Copilot suggestions with manual implementations.

Answer: B

Explanation: By providing comments that explicitly state the need for input sanitization or validation, Copilot can be guided to generate safe and secure suggestions, reducing the risk of injection attacks or unsafe practices.

462. How can Copilot assist in optimizing recursive algorithms for large datasets?

A) By disabling recursion and suggesting iterative approaches.

B) By suggesting memoization techniques to avoid redundant calculations.

C) By automating recursion for all data-processing tasks.

D) By limiting recursion depth in all suggested algorithms.

Answer: B

Explanation: Recursive algorithms can be inefficient for large datasets due to repeated calculations. Copilot can suggest memoization techniques, which store intermediate results, significantly improving performance and reducing computational overhead.

463. How does Copilot handle debugging code with dynamic typing, such as in Python?

A) By enforcing strict type hints in all suggestions.

B) By suggesting runtime type checks and annotations for critical variables.

C) By replacing dynamically typed constructs with statically typed alternatives.

D) By automating variable type inference.

Answer: B

Explanation: Copilot can suggest runtime type checks and optional type annotations to improve code robustness in dynamically typed languages like Python, helping catch type-related errors earlier in the development process.

464. What is a key advantage of using Copilot for debugging event-driven architectures?

A) It automates all event handler functions.

B) It suggests fixes for race conditions and missed event triggers.

C) It disables unused events in the architecture.

D) It replaces event-driven models with synchronous flows.

Answer: B

Explanation: Event-driven architectures often face issues like race conditions or missed triggers. Copilot can suggest thread-safe mechanisms and logic corrections to ensure reliable event handling and improve system stability.

465. How can Copilot assist in debugging misaligned serialization formats between microservices?

A) By automating serialization and deserialization workflows.

B) By suggesting fixes for mismatched schema definitions and serialization logic.

C) By replacing serialization with raw data transmission.

D) By disabling unsupported serialization formats.

Answer: B

Explanation: Serialization mismatches between microservices can lead to runtime errors. Copilot can suggest schema corrections or alignment with standard serialization formats, ensuring compatibility between services.

466. What troubleshooting step should you take if Copilot generates inefficient database query suggestions?

A) Disable Copilot for database-related tasks.

B) Refine comments to specify optimization constraints, such as indexing or limiting rows.

C) Automate query generation for all database operations.

D) Replace Copilot-generated queries with manual SQL.

Answer: B

Explanation: Providing precise comments about indexing, query limits, or expected results helps Copilot generate efficient database queries, avoiding performance bottlenecks or unnecessary computations.

467. How can Copilot assist in debugging state inconsistencies in Redux-based applications?

A) By disabling state changes in reducers.

B) By suggesting fixes for incorrect action handling or reducer logic.

C) By replacing Redux with simpler state management libraries.

D) By automating all state updates.

Answer: B

Explanation: Copilot can identify issues in Redux-based applications, such as incorrect action types or faulty reducer logic, and suggest improvements to maintain predictable and consistent state updates.

468. What is the practical use of Copilot in debugging deadlocks in concurrent systems?

A) Automating deadlock detection in multi-threaded environments.

B) Suggesting proper lock acquisition order and timeout mechanisms.

C) Disabling concurrency features in the codebase.

D) Replacing locks with polling mechanisms.

Answer: B

Explanation: Deadlocks occur when threads wait indefinitely for resources. Copilot can suggest proper lock acquisition order or timeout mechanisms, reducing the likelihood of deadlocks and improving system reliability.

469. How does Copilot assist in debugging polyglot microservices that use multiple programming languages?

A) By suggesting language-agnostic solutions for common patterns like API communication.

B) By disabling language-specific constructs in the codebase.

C) By automating the translation of code between languages.

D) By replacing polyglot architecture with monolithic design.

Answer: A

Explanation: In polyglot microservices, Copilot can suggest language-agnostic solutions for API communication, serialization, and data exchange, ensuring interoperability and reducing cross-language friction.

470. What is the role of Copilot in troubleshooting DevOps pipeline failures caused by environment misconfigurations?

A) Automating environment setup for all pipelines.

B) Suggesting fixes for missing environment variables and invalid dependency paths.

C) Disabling affected pipeline stages.

D) Replacing environment-specific workflows with generic ones.

Answer: B

Explanation: Copilot can identify and resolve issues such as missing environment variables, incorrect file paths, or dependency configurations, minimizing pipeline failures and improving reliability.

471. How can Copilot assist in debugging infinite loops in functional programming?

A) By suggesting termination conditions for recursive functions or lazy evaluations.

B) By automating loop unrolling for all iterations.

C) By replacing functional constructs with imperative ones.

D) By disabling recursive functions entirely.

Answer: A

Explanation: Infinite loops in functional programming often result from missing termination conditions. Copilot can suggest appropriate base cases or conditions for lazy evaluations to ensure termination.

472. What is a recommended way to use Copilot for debugging deeply nested JSON data structures?

A) Automate JSON parsing for all nested structures.

B) Suggest helper functions for extracting and validating nested keys.

C) Disable JSON handling in the codebase.

D) Replace nested structures with flat data models.

Answer: B

Explanation: Copilot can suggest helper functions or utilities for extracting and validating keys in deeply nested JSON structures, simplifying debugging and improving data handling.

473. How does Copilot assist in debugging pipeline failures caused by version mismatches in dependencies?

A) By automating dependency updates for all stages.

B) By suggesting compatible versions and resolving conflicts in dependency files.

C) By disabling unsupported dependencies.

D) By replacing dependencies with built-in library functions.

Answer: B

Explanation: Copilot can analyze dependency files like package.json or requirements.txt and suggest compatible versions or conflict resolutions, reducing failures caused by version mismatches.

474. How can Copilot help troubleshoot incorrect data bindings in reactive UI frameworks like Angular?

A) Automating data binding generation.

B) Suggesting fixes for invalid property binding or syntax.

C) Disabling two-way data binding in the framework.

D) Replacing reactive constructs with static templates.

Answer: B

Explanation: Incorrect data bindings can break UI functionality. Copilot can identify and correct issues like invalid property names, missing directives, or incorrect syntax in reactive frameworks.

475. What is the practical use of Copilot in debugging network latency issues in distributed systems?

A) By automating network retries for all operations.

B) By suggesting improvements to retry logic, timeouts, and circuit breakers.

C) By disabling distributed workflows.

D) By replacing network calls with local operations.

Answer: B

Explanation: Copilot can suggest optimizations such as retry logic, timeout configurations, or circuit-breaker patterns to manage network latency and improve system resilience.

476. How can Copilot assist in debugging containerized applications with faulty configurations?

A) By automating container orchestration.

B) By suggesting fixes for misconfigured Dockerfile or Kubernetes manifests.

C) By disabling affected containers in the cluster.

D) By replacing containerized applications with virtual machines.

Answer: B

Explanation: Copilot can analyze configuration files like Dockerfile or Kubernetes manifests and suggest corrections to issues like missing environment variables, incorrect ports, or invalid syntax.

477. What is a recommended way to guide Copilot when troubleshooting logic errors in functional programming?

A) Disabling Copilot for functional constructs.

B) Adding detailed comments about expected input-output relationships and constraints.

C) Automating all functional tests.

D) Replacing functional programming with imperative constructs.

Answer: B

Explanation: Providing detailed comments about input-output relationships helps Copilot generate logic that adheres to functional programming principles and avoids errors.

478. How does Copilot assist in debugging permission errors in cloud-based DevOps pipelines?

A) Automating permission management for all pipelines.

B) Suggesting fixes for misconfigured access roles and policies.

C) Disabling affected pipeline stages.

D) Replacing cloud-based workflows with local ones.

Answer: B

Explanation: Permission errors often result from misconfigured access roles or policies. Copilot can analyze IAM configurations and suggest fixes to resolve these issues.

479. How can Copilot assist in troubleshooting memory fragmentation in low-level programming?

A) Automating memory allocation for all variables.

B) Suggesting efficient memory allocation and deallocation strategies.

C) Disabling dynamic memory usage in the codebase.

D) Replacing low-level code with high-level abstractions.

Answer: B

Explanation: Memory fragmentation can degrade performance in low-level programming. Copilot can suggest optimized allocation and deallocation strategies to reduce fragmentation and improve efficiency.

Domain 9: Open Source and Educational Use Cases

480. How can GitHub Copilot assist in contributing to an open-source project with minimal documentation?

A) By automating pull request approvals.

B) By suggesting code snippets based on existing patterns in the project.

C) By disabling contributions to poorly documented projects.

D) By replacing manual contributions with AI-driven workflows.

Answer: B

Explanation: Copilot analyzes existing patterns in the project's codebase and generates relevant suggestions, even when documentation is sparse, enabling contributors to maintain consistency with the project's style.

481. What is a key limitation of using Copilot for legacy codebases?

A) Copilot cannot analyze large files.

B) Copilot struggles with identifying the intent behind poorly documented or outdated code.

C) Copilot cannot generate suggestions for object-oriented programming.

D) Copilot disables suggestions for legacy formats.

Explanation: Legacy codebases often lack modern best practices and adequate documentation, making it challenging for Copilot to accurately understand the code's intent and provide meaningful suggestions.

482. How can Copilot help developers learn a new programming language?

A) By automating all language-specific tasks.

B) By suggesting idiomatic code patterns and explaining syntax.

C) By disabling features for unsupported languages.

D) By generating compliance certificates for language proficiency.

Answer: B

Explanation: Copilot can suggest idiomatic code patterns and provide context-aware examples, helping developers understand syntax and best practices in a new programming language.

483. What is a best practice when using Copilot for educational projects?

A) Automate all project workflows with Copilot.

B) Use Copilot-generated code as a learning tool while reviewing and understanding its suggestions.

C) Replace manual learning with AI-driven project development.

D) Disable Copilot in educational settings.

Answer: B

Explanation: Copilot-generated code should be reviewed and understood to ensure it aligns with learning objectives, making it a valuable tool for educational projects.

484. How can Copilot assist in debugging open-source projects written in unfamiliar frameworks?

A) By automating framework-specific testing workflows.

B) By suggesting fixes based on the framework's conventions and patterns.

C) By disabling suggestions for unsupported frameworks.

D) By generating compliance reports for open-source contributions.

Answer: B

Explanation: Copilot leverages its knowledge of various frameworks to suggest fixes and improvements that align with their conventions, simplifying debugging in unfamiliar environments.

485. What is a limitation when using Copilot for personal projects with custom logic?

A) Copilot cannot generate suggestions for custom algorithms.

B) Copilot may not fully understand unique project-specific logic without sufficient context.

C) Copilot disables suggestions for personal repositories.

D) Copilot replaces manual coding in personal projects.

Answer: B

Explanation: Copilot relies on context to generate meaningful suggestions. For custom logic, developers may need to provide detailed comments or examples to guide Copilot effectively.

486. How can Copilot support collaborative open-source development?

A) By automating code reviews for all contributors.

B) By providing consistent coding patterns and styles across contributions.

C) By replacing manual pull requests with AI-generated workflows.

D) By disabling conflicting contributions automatically.

Answer: B

Explanation: Copilot ensures consistency in coding patterns and styles, making it easier for contributors to align their work with the project's standards and maintain code quality.

487. What is a practical use of Copilot in learning a new web development framework like React?

A) Automating all component creation.

B) Suggesting boilerplate code for components and hooks while explaining their purpose.

C) Disabling advanced features in the framework.

D) Replacing manual reading of framework documentation.

Answer: B

Explanation: Copilot can generate boilerplate code for components and hooks, providing explanations that help developers understand the framework's core concepts and best practices.

488. How does Copilot handle poorly documented legacy APIs in an open-source project?

A) By automating API integration workflows.

B) By suggesting API calls based on observed patterns in the codebase.

C) By disabling API-related suggestions.

D) By replacing legacy APIs with modern ones.

Answer: B

Explanation: Copilot observes patterns in the existing codebase and generates API call suggestions that align with those patterns, even when documentation is inadequate.

489. What is a limitation of using Copilot for multi-language educational projects?

A) Copilot disables suggestions for secondary languages.

B) Copilot may struggle to provide accurate suggestions when switching contexts between languages.

C) Copilot replaces secondary languages with primary ones.

D) Copilot generates compliance reports for all languages.

Answer: B

Explanation: Switching between multiple languages in a single project can reduce Copilot's context accuracy, making it harder to generate relevant suggestions without sufficient guidance.

490. How can Copilot assist in writing unit tests for open-source contributions?

A) By automating test execution.

B) By generating test cases based on observed input-output patterns in the existing code.

C) By disabling test generation for unsupported frameworks.

D) By replacing manual testing workflows.

Answer: B

Explanation: Copilot can analyze existing input-output patterns in the codebase and generate relevant unit test cases, making it easier for contributors to validate their changes.

491. What is a practical use of Copilot in debugging educational projects?

A) Automating the entire debugging process.

B) Suggesting fixes for common issues while explaining the underlying problem.

C) Disabling debugging for educational codebases.

D) Replacing manual debugging with AI-driven workflows.

Answer: B

Explanation: Copilot can identify common issues in educational projects and suggest fixes, providing explanations that help learners understand the cause of the problem and how to resolve it.

492. How can Copilot support learning a new database query language like SQL?

A) Automating all query execution.

B) Generating optimized queries and explaining their syntax and structure.

C) Disabling advanced features in the language.

D) Replacing manual database operations with AI-driven queries.

Answer: B

Explanation: Copilot can generate optimized SQL queries and provide explanations for their syntax and structure, helping learners understand best practices in query writing.

493. What is a common challenge when using Copilot for personal projects with unconventional programming paradigms?

A) Copilot disables suggestions for unconventional paradigms.

B) Copilot may generate suggestions that do not align with the project's unique paradigms.

C) Copilot replaces unconventional paradigms with standard ones.

D) Copilot automates all workflows in the project.

Answer: B

Explanation: Unconventional programming paradigms may not align with Copilot's training data, leading to suggestions that require additional validation or customization by the developer.

494. How can Copilot assist in understanding poorly documented open-source libraries?

A) Automating library integration workflows.

B) Suggesting usage examples based on existing patterns in the codebase.

C) Disabling library-related suggestions.

D) Replacing poorly documented libraries with modern alternatives.

Answer: B

Explanation: Copilot can analyze the codebase and suggest usage examples for poorly documented libraries, helping developers understand how to integrate and use them effectively.

495. What is a key advantage of using Copilot for collaborative educational projects?

A) Automating all contributions.

B) Ensuring coding style consistency across contributors.

C) Disabling conflicting contributions automatically.

D) Replacing manual collaboration with AI-driven workflows.

Answer: B

Explanation: Copilot helps ensure consistency in coding styles and best practices, making it easier for teams to collaborate effectively on educational projects.

496. How does Copilot support learning functional programming in languages like Haskell or Scala?

A) Automating all functional constructs.

B) Suggesting idiomatic patterns like higher-order functions and pure functions.

C) Disabling advanced features in the language.

D) Replacing functional constructs with imperative ones.

Answer: B

Explanation: Copilot provides idiomatic patterns and examples, such as higher-order functions and pure functions, helping learners adopt functional programming principles in languages like Haskell or Scala.

497. How can Copilot assist in resolving dependency conflicts in open-source projects?

A) Automating dependency resolution for all projects.

B) Suggesting compatible versions and conflict resolutions for dependency files.

C) Disabling unsupported dependencies automatically.

D) Replacing dependency management with manual workflows.

Answer: B

Explanation: Copilot analyzes dependency files like package.json or requirements.txt and suggests compatible versions or conflict resolutions, simplifying dependency management in open-source projects.

498. What is a limitation of using Copilot for learning a new framework with limited documentation?

A) Copilot disables suggestions for undocumented frameworks.

B) Copilot may generate incomplete or contextually inaccurate suggestions.

C) Copilot replaces undocumented frameworks with modern alternatives.

D) Copilot automates all workflows for undocumented frameworks.

Answer: B

Explanation: Limited documentation can reduce Copilot's ability to provide accurate suggestions, requiring developers to validate and adapt its outputs for the framework.

499. How can Copilot improve efficiency in educational projects with repetitive tasks?

A) Automating all repetitive tasks without validation.

B) Generating boilerplate code for repetitive patterns and structures.

C) Disabling repetitive tasks in the project.

D) Replacing manual workflows with AI-driven automation.

Answer: B

Explanation: Copilot simplifies repetitive tasks by generating boilerplate code for common patterns and structures, allowing learners to focus on understanding core concepts.

500. How can Copilot help in understanding the structure of a large open-source monorepo?

A) By automating the navigation of all files.

B) By suggesting entry points and high-level overviews based on the project structure.

C) By disabling complex features in monorepos.

D) By replacing manual exploration with AI-driven workflows.

Answer: B

Explanation: Large open-source monorepos can be overwhelming to navigate. Copilot analyzes the structure and provides suggestions for entry points or key modules, helping developers quickly understand the project's organization.

501. How can Copilot assist educators in creating coding exercises for students?

A) By automating the grading process for all exercises.

B) By generating starter code and problem statements aligned with specific learning objectives.

C) By disabling manual teaching workflows.

D) By replacing traditional exercises with AI-driven examples.

Answer: B

Explanation: Copilot can generate starter code and tailored problem statements, making it easier for educators to design exercises that align with specific programming concepts or learning objectives.

502. What is a key challenge when using Copilot for poorly documented open-source libraries?

A) Copilot cannot generate suggestions for libraries with missing documentation.

B) Copilot may suggest incorrect or incomplete usage patterns without sufficient context.

C) Copilot disables suggestions for undocumented libraries.

D) Copilot replaces poorly documented libraries with modern alternatives.

Answer: B

Explanation: Without sufficient documentation, Copilot relies solely on observed patterns in the codebase, which could lead to incomplete or incorrect suggestions. Validation by the developer is essential in such cases.

503. How can Copilot help students learn debugging techniques in their educational projects?

A) By automating the resolution of all bugs.

B) By suggesting fixes for common errors and explaining the cause of the issue.

C) By disabling debugging workflows in educational projects.

D) By replacing manual debugging with AI-driven automation.

Answer: B

Explanation: Copilot can identify common errors in code and suggest fixes while providing explanations for the root cause, helping students learn effective debugging techniques.

504. What is a best practice for using Copilot in personal projects exploring experimental programming paradigms?

A) Automating all experimental workflows.

B) Providing detailed comments to guide Copilot in generating paradigm-specific suggestions.

C) Disabling Copilot for experimental projects.

D) Replacing experimental paradigms with standard practices.

Answer: B

Explanation: Experimental paradigms often require precise guidance. Adding detailed comments ensures that Copilot generates suggestions aligned with the specific paradigm being explored.

505. How can Copilot assist in resolving version mismatches between dependencies in an open-source project?

A) By automating dependency updates.

B) By suggesting compatible versions and highlighting conflicts in dependency files.

C) By disabling unsupported dependencies automatically.

D) By replacing dependency management with static references.

Answer: B

Explanation: Copilot analyzes dependency files and suggests compatible versions or resolutions for conflicts, reducing the effort needed to address version mismatches in open-source projects.

506. How does Copilot support learning advanced concepts in a new programming language?

A) By automating the implementation of all advanced concepts.

B) By generating examples that demonstrate advanced features like closures or metaprogramming.

C) By disabling advanced features in the language.

D) By replacing manual learning with AI-driven automation.

Answer: B

Explanation: Copilot can generate examples showcasing advanced features, such as closures or metaprogramming, helping learners understand and apply these concepts in real-world scenarios.

507. What is the practical limitation of using Copilot for contributing to open-source projects with unconventional code styles?

A) Copilot disables suggestions for unconventional code styles.

B) Copilot may generate suggestions that do not align with the project's unique style guidelines.

C) Copilot replaces unconventional styles with standard ones.

D) Copilot automates all style enforcement workflows.

Answer: B

Explanation: Unconventional code styles might not align with Copilot's training data, leading to suggestions that require manual adaptation to fit the project's style guidelines.

508. How does Copilot assist in creating interactive educational projects?

A) By automating all interactive workflows.

B) By generating boilerplate code for interactive features like forms or animations.

C) By disabling interactivity in educational projects.

D) By replacing interactive elements with static templates.

Answer: B

Explanation: Copilot can provide boilerplate code for interactive features, such as forms, animations, or real-time data updates, enabling students to focus on enhancing their projects' core functionality.

509. How can Copilot be effectively used in open-source projects that rely heavily on test-driven development (TDD)?

A) By automating all test cases.

B) By generating test cases before implementation and aligning them with TDD principles.

C) By disabling testing workflows for TDD projects.

D) By replacing manual testing with AI-driven automation.

Answer: B

Explanation: In TDD, tests are written before the actual code. Copilot can generate test cases aligned with specified requirements, helping maintain adherence to TDD principles in open-source development.

510. What is the limitation of using Copilot for educational projects involving legacy technologies?

A) Copilot disables suggestions for legacy technologies.

B) Copilot may struggle to provide accurate suggestions due to limited modern context for outdated technologies.

C) Copilot replaces legacy technologies with modern alternatives.

D) Copilot automates all workflows for legacy technologies.

Answer: B

Explanation: Legacy technologies often lack modern best practices or sufficient training examples for Copilot, leading to suggestions that may require additional validation or manual refinement.

511. How can Copilot assist in refactoring poorly documented open-source projects?

A) By automating the entire refactoring process.

B) By suggesting improvements to code readability and modularization.

C) By disabling refactoring for undocumented projects.

D) By replacing the codebase with a modern alternative.

Answer: B

Explanation: Copilot can suggest ways to improve code readability, modularization, and maintainability, even in poorly documented projects, helping contributors refactor code effectively.

512. How does Copilot support students in learning web technologies like HTML, CSS, and JavaScript?

A) By automating the creation of all web pages.

B) By generating examples for layouts, animations, and interactivity with explanations.

C) By disabling advanced features in web technologies.

D) By replacing manual learning with AI-driven automation.

Answer: B

Explanation: Copilot can generate examples for responsive layouts, animations, and interactive elements, helping students understand and apply web technologies effectively in their projects.

513. What is a key advantage of using Copilot for collaborative educational hackathons?

A) Automating all contributions from participants.

B) Maintaining project consistency by providing standard coding patterns.

C) Disabling conflicting contributions automatically.

D) Replacing manual collaboration with AI-driven workflows.

Answer: B

Explanation: Consistency in coding patterns and styles is critical in collaborative projects like hackathons. Copilot ensures that contributions from different participants align with project standards.

514. How can Copilot assist in understanding complex algorithms in open-source projects?

A) By automating the execution of all algorithms.

B) By providing simplified explanations and alternative implementations.

C) By disabling algorithm-related suggestions in the project.

D) By replacing complex algorithms with standard ones.

Answer: B

Explanation: Copilot can generate alternative implementations or simplified explanations for complex algorithms, helping contributors understand and adapt them to their use cases.

515. What is a practical way to use Copilot for debugging code in educational projects using new frameworks?

A) Automating all debugging workflows.

B) Suggesting fixes for common issues and framework-specific best practices.

C) Disabling debugging workflows for new frameworks.

D) Replacing frameworks with simpler alternatives.

Answer: B

Explanation: Copilot can provide fixes for common framework-specific issues, helping students debug their code while learning best practices for the new framework.

516. How can Copilot assist in contributing to multilingual open-source projects?

A) Automating all contributions in secondary languages.

B) Generating context-aware suggestions for each language in the project.

C) Disabling contributions in non-primary languages.

D) Replacing multilingual workflows with single-language approaches.

Answer: B

Explanation: Copilot provides context-aware suggestions tailored to each language in multilingual projects, enabling contributors to work effectively across multiple languages.

517. How does Copilot support learning data visualization libraries like D3.js or Matplotlib?

A) Automating the creation of all visualizations.

B) Suggesting code for common visualization patterns and explaining their structure.

C) Disabling advanced features in visualization libraries.

D) Replacing manual visualization workflows with AI-driven automation.

Answer: B

Explanation: Copilot can generate code for common visualization patterns, such as bar charts or scatter plots, and explain their structure, helping learners understand how to use data visualization libraries effectively.

518. What is a key limitation of using Copilot for open-source projects with sparse commit histories?

A) Copilot disables suggestions for projects with sparse commit histories.

B) Copilot may struggle to analyze patterns due to the lack of sufficient historical data.

C) Copilot replaces sparse commit histories with synthetic data.

D) Copilot automates all workflows for such projects.

Answer: B

Explanation: Sparse commit histories provide limited context for Copilot to analyze, which may reduce the relevance of its suggestions for open-source projects.

519. How can Copilot simplify learning domain-specific languages (DSLs) used in open-source projects?

A) By automating all DSL-related workflows.

B) By generating examples of DSL usage with explanations for domain-specific concepts.

C) By disabling DSL-related suggestions.

D) By replacing DSLs with general-purpose languages.

Answer: B

Explanation: Copilot can generate examples and explanations for DSLs, helping learners understand and apply domain-specific concepts in open-source projects.

520. How can Copilot assist in understanding a project's dependency graph in an open-source repository?

A) By automating dependency installation.

B) By suggesting visualizations of dependencies based on configuration files like package.json.

C) By disabling unsupported dependencies automatically.

D) By replacing dependency graphs with a simplified list.

Answer: B

Explanation: Copilot can parse dependency configuration files (e.g., package.json, requirements.txt) and suggest visualizations or summaries of how modules interact. This helps contributors understand the project's structure and dependencies more effectively.

521. What is a key challenge when using Copilot to learn legacy frameworks no longer actively maintained?

A) Copilot disables suggestions for legacy frameworks.

B) Copilot may suggest outdated patterns that don't align with modern practices.

C) Copilot replaces legacy patterns with modern alternatives.

D) Copilot automates the migration of legacy frameworks.

Answer: B

Explanation: Legacy frameworks often have outdated patterns and practices. While Copilot can suggest code, these suggestions may not align with modern security or performance standards, requiring additional validation.

522. How can educators leverage Copilot to introduce students to error-handling best practices?

A) By automating error resolution in all exercises.

B) By generating examples of common error-handling patterns with explanations.

C) By disabling error-related suggestions in exercises.

D) By replacing manual error handling with AI-driven workflows.

Answer: B

Explanation: Copilot can generate examples of effective error-handling patterns, such as try-catch blocks, exception handling, or validations. Educators can use these examples to teach students how to write robust and error-resistant code.

523. How can Copilot assist in contributing to open-source projects with strict coding style requirements?

A) By automating style enforcement for all contributions.

B) By suggesting code snippets that comply with predefined style guidelines.

C) By disabling suggestions for unsupported code styles.

D) By replacing manual contributions with pre-validated styles.

Answer: B

Explanation: Copilot can analyze the repository's codebase and suggest snippets adhering to its coding style, ensuring that contributions follow the project's standards without requiring extensive manual adjustments.

524. How can Copilot support learning a new asynchronous programming model like in Node.js?

A) By automating all asynchronous workflows.

B) By generating examples of promises, async/await, and callbacks with explanations.

C) By disabling asynchronous constructs in the codebase.

D) By replacing asynchronous programming with synchronous examples.

Answer: B

Explanation: Copilot can provide examples of different asynchronous paradigms (e.g., promises, async/await) and explain their usage, helping learners understand how to handle asynchronous code effectively in Node.js or similar environments.

525. What is a limitation of using Copilot to debug open-source projects with minimal test coverage?

A) Copilot disables debugging workflows for untested projects.

B) Copilot may fail to suggest fixes without sufficient test cases to validate behavior.

C) Copilot replaces manual debugging with automated workflows.

D) Copilot automates test case generation for all scenarios.

Answer: B

Explanation: Without test coverage, Copilot lacks the context needed to validate its suggestions, making it harder to debug effectively. Developers must manually verify the accuracy of Copilot's recommendations in such cases.

526. How can Copilot assist in refactoring educational projects that use procedural programming?

A) By automating the entire refactoring process.

B) By suggesting modularized code and transitioning to object-oriented or functional styles.

C) By disabling refactoring suggestions for procedural code.

D) By replacing procedural code with modern libraries.

Answer: B

Explanation: Copilot can analyze procedural code and suggest ways to modularize it, such as breaking it into functions or transitioning to object-oriented or functional programming styles, improving maintainability and scalability.

527. What is a practical way to use Copilot for exploring new design patterns in educational projects?

A) By automating design pattern implementation.

B) By generating examples of patterns like Singleton, Factory, or Observer with explanations.

C) By disabling unsupported design patterns.

D) By replacing manual implementation with pre-built patterns.

Answer: B

Explanation: Copilot can generate examples of popular design patterns and explain their use cases, helping students understand how to apply these patterns to solve common software design challenges.

528. How can Copilot assist in debugging poorly formatted configuration files in open-source projects?

A) By automating file formatting for all configurations.

B) By suggesting corrections for syntax errors and formatting issues.

C) By disabling suggestions for configuration files.

D) By replacing manual corrections with pre-validated templates.

Answer: B

Explanation: Copilot can identify syntax errors or misconfigurations in files like YAML, JSON, or XML and suggest corrections, speeding up the debugging process for configuration-related issues.

529. What is a key benefit of using Copilot to learn a framework like Django for web development?

A) By automating the creation of entire web applications.

B) By generating boilerplate code for models, views, and templates with explanations.

C) By disabling advanced features in the framework.

D) By replacing manual learning with AI-driven tutorials.

Answer: B

Explanation: Copilot can generate boilerplate code for common Django components (e.g., models, views, templates) and explain their purpose, helping learners understand the framework's architecture and workflow.

530. How can Copilot assist in contributing to open-source projects with multilingual documentation?

A) By automating translation of all documentation.

B) By suggesting consistent terminology across different languages.

C) By disabling multilingual documentation contributions.

D) By replacing documentation with a single language.

Answer: B

Explanation: Copilot can provide terminology suggestions that ensure consistency across multilingual documentation, helping contributors maintain clarity and uniformity in open-source projects.

531. How can Copilot support students in learning data analysis libraries like Pandas or NumPy?

A) By automating all data analysis workflows.

B) By generating examples for operations like filtering, aggregation, and reshaping data with explanations.

C) By disabling unsupported operations in data analysis libraries.

D) By replacing manual operations with pre-built solutions.

Answer: B

Explanation: Copilot can generate examples for common data analysis tasks, such as filtering or aggregating data, and explain the syntax and logic, helping students gain practical experience with libraries like Pandas or NumPy.

532. How does Copilot assist in debugging dependency injection issues in educational projects?

A) By automating dependency injection for all classes.

B) By suggesting fixes for circular dependencies and misconfigured injections.

C) By disabling dependency injection in educational contexts.

D) By replacing dependency injection with static references.

Answer: B

Explanation: Copilot identifies issues like circular dependencies or incorrect configurations in dependency injection frameworks and suggests fixes, helping students learn this complex concept more effectively.

533. How can Copilot be used to identify unused code in open-source contributions?

A) By automating unused code removal.

B) By suggesting code that is not invoked or referenced within the repository.

C) By disabling suggestions for redundant code.

D) By replacing unused code with placeholders.

Answer: B

Explanation: Copilot can analyze the codebase and highlight snippets that are never invoked or referenced, helping contributors clean up unused code and improve maintainability.

534. What is a practical challenge when using Copilot to debug multi-threaded programs in educational projects?

A) Copilot disables multi-threaded suggestions.

B) Copilot may not fully understand concurrency issues like race conditions or deadlocks.

C) Copilot replaces multi-threading with single-threaded examples.

D) Copilot automates debugging for all concurrency issues.

Answer: B

Explanation: Debugging concurrency issues requires a deep understanding of shared resource access and synchronization. While Copilot can suggest solutions, these may require additional manual validation to ensure correctness.

Domain 10: Scenario-Based Questions with Coding Contexts

535. Scenario: You are contributing to an open-source project that uses a custom-built logging library. The library lacks sufficient documentation.

Question: How can Copilot assist you in adding a new logging feature to this library?

A) By automating the implementation of all logging features.

B) By suggesting code snippets based on the logging patterns observed in the existing library.

C) By replacing the custom library with a modern logging framework.

D) By disabling suggestions for undocumented libraries.

Answer: B

Explanation: Copilot analyzes the existing patterns in the custom library and generates suggestions aligned with the observed functionality, even in the absence of documentation.

536. Scenario: You are learning a new functional programming language and need to implement a higher-order function that applies a transformation to a list of numbers.

Question: How does Copilot help you achieve this?

A) By automating the entire higher-order function implementation.

B) By generating examples of applying transformations using map or lambda functions.

C) By replacing higher-order functions with imperative loops.

D) By disabling functional programming constructs.

Answer: B

Explanation: Copilot provides examples of idiomatic usage of higher-order functions like map or filter, demonstrating how transformations can be applied to elements in a list.

537. Scenario: Your educational project involves creating an interactive quiz app using JavaScript. You need to dynamically update the score on the webpage.

Question: How can Copilot assist in implementing this feature?

A) By automating the entire quiz application.

B) By suggesting JavaScript code to update DOM elements dynamically based on user interactions.

C) By disabling interactivity features in the project.

D) By replacing manual DOM manipulation with static templates.

Answer: B

Explanation: Copilot can suggest JavaScript code that uses methods like document.querySelector and innerHTML to update the DOM dynamically, making the score update seamless.

538. Scenario: You are contributing to an open-source project written in Python, and you find that the project lacks sufficient unit tests.

Question: How can Copilot assist in improving the test coverage?

A) By automating test execution workflows.

B) By suggesting unit test cases for functions based on their input-output patterns.

C) By replacing manual testing with pre-built templates.

D) By disabling testing workflows for the project.

Answer: B

Explanation: Copilot analyzes the function definitions and suggests test cases that align with commonly expected input-output behaviors, improving test coverage.

539. Scenario: You are tasked with refactoring a legacy open-source project that uses procedural code. The goal is to make it modular and reusable.

Question: How can Copilot help with this refactoring effort?

A) By automating the entire modularization process.

B) By suggesting ways to break down large functions into smaller, reusable modules.

C) By replacing the legacy code with a modern library.

D) By disabling procedural programming constructs.

Answer: B

Explanation: Copilot identifies opportunities for modularization by suggesting how to decompose large functions into smaller, reusable components, improving maintainability.

540. Scenario: Your team is building an educational platform, and you need to implement a feature that tracks user activity on the platform.

Question: How can Copilot assist in implementing this tracking feature?

A) By automating the user activity tracking for all features.

B) By suggesting boilerplate code for event listeners to capture user interactions.

C) By replacing tracking features with static analytics.

D) By disabling user interaction tracking.

Answer: B

Explanation: Copilot generates boilerplate code for event listeners, enabling you to capture user interactions like clicks and form submissions for activity tracking.

541. Scenario: You are exploring a new object-oriented programming language and need to implement an inheritance hierarchy for a vehicle system.

Question: How can Copilot assist in this task?

A) By automating the creation of all classes and methods.

B) By suggesting class definitions and inheritance structures for vehicles like cars and trucks.

C) By replacing inheritance with procedural code.

D) By disabling object-oriented features in the language.

Answer: B

Explanation: Copilot provides suggestions for class hierarchies, including parent and child relationships, showcasing how to implement inheritance effectively in the new language.

542. Scenario: You are debugging an open-source project that uses asynchronous APIs, and you encounter race conditions.

Question: How does Copilot help resolve this issue?

A) By automating the debugging of all asynchronous workflows.

B) By suggesting solutions like locks, semaphores, or proper async/await usage.

C) By replacing asynchronous APIs with synchronous equivalents.

D) By disabling asynchronous features in the project.

Answer: B

Explanation: Copilot identifies potential race conditions and suggests thread-safe mechanisms or improved async/await constructs to resolve concurrency issues.

543. Scenario: You want to implement a multi-language support feature in your educational app.

Question: How can Copilot assist in building this feature?

A) By automating translation for all content.

B) By suggesting code for language selection and loading localized resources.

C) By replacing multi-language support with a single language.

D) By disabling multi-language features in the app.

Answer: B

Explanation: Copilot can generate code for switching languages (e.g., dropdown selection) and loading appropriate localized resources, enabling multi-language support efficiently.

544. Scenario: You are contributing to an open-source machine learning project, and you need to preprocess a dataset with missing values.

Question: How does Copilot help with this preprocessing task?

A) By automating the entire preprocessing pipeline.

B) By suggesting techniques like imputing missing values or dropping incomplete rows.

C) By replacing missing values with default settings.

D) By disabling preprocessing workflows.

Answer: B

Explanation: Copilot can suggest data preprocessing techniques, such as imputing missing values with the mean or median, or filtering rows, ensuring the dataset is clean for machine learning tasks.

545. Scenario: You are learning a new framework like Flask for building web applications and need to create a REST API.

Question: How can Copilot assist in generating the REST API?

A) By automating the creation of the entire web application.

B) By suggesting boilerplate code for endpoints, including GET, POST, and DELETE methods.

C) By disabling advanced features in Flask.

D) By replacing REST APIs with static web pages.

Answer: B

Explanation: Copilot provides boilerplate examples for REST API endpoints, demonstrating how to handle HTTP methods and integrate them with the Flask framework.

546. Scenario: You are contributing to an open-source project that uses CI/CD pipelines, and one of the build stages is failing due to a misconfigured environment variable.

Question: How does Copilot help resolve this issue?

A) By automating the entire CI/CD pipeline.

B) By suggesting corrections for misconfigured variables in build scripts or configuration files.

C) By disabling the failing build stage.

D) By replacing CI/CD workflows with manual builds.

Answer: B

Explanation: Copilot suggests fixes for environment variables in build scripts, ensuring that the pipeline has the correct configurations to proceed successfully.

547. Scenario: Your educational project involves visualizing real-time data using JavaScript.

Question: How can Copilot assist in implementing this visualization?

A) By automating all data visualization workflows.

B) By suggesting code for rendering real-time graphs using libraries like Chart.js or D3.js.

C) By replacing real-time data with static charts.

D) By disabling visualization features in the project.

Answer: B

Explanation: Copilot provides code examples for integrating libraries like Chart.js to render real-time graphs, enabling visualization of dynamic data effectively.

548. Scenario: You are building a chatbot for an open-source educational project and need to integrate natural language processing (NLP).

Question: How does Copilot help with this integration?

A) By automating all NLP workflows.

B) By suggesting code for tokenization, sentiment analysis, or intent classification.

C) By replacing NLP features with static responses.

D) By disabling NLP features in the chatbot.

Answer: B

Explanation: Copilot suggests code for common NLP tasks, such as tokenizing input text or performing sentiment analysis, helping you build an intelligent chatbot.

549. Scenario: You are contributing to an open-source project with minimal frontend documentation and need to add a new UI feature.

Question: How can Copilot assist in this scenario?

A) By automating the entire frontend development.

B) By suggesting frontend code snippets based on existing patterns in the project.

C) By replacing the existing UI framework with a new one.

D) By disabling frontend feature suggestions.

Answer: B

Explanation: Copilot analyzes the current UI patterns and generates suggestions for new features that align with the existing framework, even in the absence of detailed documentation.

550. Scenario: You are contributing to an open-source project, and you need to squash multiple commits into a single commit.

Question: What Git command should you use to squash commits?

A) git merge --squash

B) git rebase -i HEAD~n

C) git reset --soft

D) git commit --amend

Answer: B

Explanation: The git rebase -i HEAD~n command opens an interactive rebase interface where you can squash (s) multiple commits into one by editing their actions.

551. Scenario: You are debugging an issue in an open-source project hosted on GitHub and need to fetch the latest changes from the remote repository.

Question: Which Git command retrieves the latest changes without merging them?

A) git pull

B) git fetch

C) git clone

D) git rebase

Answer: B

Explanation: The git fetch command retrieves the latest changes from the remote repository but does not merge them into your local branch, allowing you to review them first.

552. Scenario: You are building a Python script for an open-source project, and it needs to handle JSON data.

Question: How can you parse a JSON string and access its data in Python?

A) Use the json.parse() method.

B) Use the json.loads() function.

C) Use the json.read() method.

D) Use the json.stringify() function.

Answer: B

Explanation: The json.loads() function in Python parses a JSON string and converts it into a Python dictionary or list, allowing you to access its data.

553. Scenario: You are contributing to an open-source Node.js project and need to install all dependencies listed in the package.json file.

Question: Which command should you run to install the dependencies?

A) npm install

B) npm update

C) npm init

D) npm run

Answer: A

Explanation: The npm install command reads the package.json file and installs all listed dependencies into the node_modules directory.

554. Scenario: Your open-source project involves Docker, and you need to build an image from a Dockerfile.

Question: Which command builds a Docker image from a Dockerfile?

A) docker run

B) docker build -t image_name .

C) docker create image_name

D) docker start image_name

Answer: B

Explanation: The docker build -t image_name . command builds a Docker image from the Dockerfile in the current directory and tags it with the specified name.

555. Scenario: You are debugging an open-source project and need to view the last 5 commits in the current branch.

Question: Which Git command should you run?

A) git show

B) git log -n 5

C) git diff HEAD~5

D) git status

Answer: B

Explanation: The git log -n 5 command displays the last 5 commits in the current branch, showing details such as commit messages and hashes.

556. Scenario: You are learning Python, and you want to create a generator function that yields even numbers up to 10.

Question: Which Python code snippet achieves this?

```
def even_generator():

    _____

    yield i
```

A) for i in range(10): if i%2==0

B) for i in range(11): if i%2==0

C) for i in range(10): if i%2!=0

D) for i in range(11): if i%2!=0

Answer: B

Explanation: The for i in range(11): if i%2==0 loop checks if i is even and yields it. Using range(11) ensures numbers up to 10 are included.

557. Scenario: You are contributing to an open-source project and need to undo the last commit without losing the changes.

Question: What Git command should you use?

A) git reset --soft HEAD^

B) git reset --hard HEAD^

C) git checkout HEAD^

D) git revert HEAD

Answer: A

Explanation: The git reset --soft HEAD^ command undoes the last commit but keeps the changes staged, allowing you to amend or modify them.

558. Scenario: You are building a simple Flask app and need to start the development server.

Question: Which command starts the Flask development server?

A) flask init

B) flask run

C) python flask start

D) python server.py

Answer: B

Explanation: The flask run command starts the Flask development server, allowing you to test your application locally.

559. Scenario: Your educational Python project requires installing the requests library.

Question: Which command should you use to install the requests library?

A) python install requests

B) pip install requests

C) pip setup requests

D) python -m requests

Answer: B

Explanation: The pip install requests command installs the requests library, which is commonly used for making HTTP requests in Python.

560. Scenario: You are learning Git and want to create a new branch called feature.

Question: What is the correct Git command to create and switch to a new branch?

A) git branch feature

B) git checkout feature

C) git checkout -b feature

D) git switch feature

Answer: C

Explanation: The git checkout -b feature command creates a new branch named feature and switches to it immediately, combining two actions in one.

561. Scenario: You need to clone an open-source repository hosted on GitHub.

Question: Which command should you use to clone the repository?

A) git clone <repository-url>

B) git pull <repository-url>

C) git fetch <repository-url>

D) git init <repository-url>

Answer: A

Explanation: The git clone <repository-url> command creates a local copy of the repository, downloading all its files and history.

562. Scenario: You are learning JavaScript and need to create an arrow function that doubles a number.

Question: Which of the following is correct?

const double = _____;

A) (x) => { return x * 2; }

B) (x) => x + 2;

C) (x) => { x * 2; }

D) (x) => return x * 2;

Answer: A

Explanation: The arrow function (x) => { return x * 2; } correctly doubles the input x. Alternatively, the shorthand (x) => x * 2 could also work.

563. Scenario: You are contributing to an open-source project and want to check which branch you are currently on.

Question: Which Git command should you use?

A) git branch

B) git status

C) git log

D) git show

Answer: A

Explanation: The git branch command lists all branches, highlighting the current one with an asterisk (*).

564. Scenario: You are debugging a Docker container that is running but not behaving as expected.

Question: Which command allows you to access the container's shell?

A) docker exec -it <container_id> /bin/bash

B) docker start <container_id>

C) docker attach <container_id>

D) docker logs <container_id>

Answer: A

Explanation: The docker exec -it <container_id> /bin/bash command opens an interactive shell inside the running container, allowing you to debug it.

565. Scenario: You are working on an open-source project and want to reset the changes in the last 3 commits but keep them in the working directory.

Question: Which Git command should you use?

A) git reset --hard HEAD~3

B) git reset --soft HEAD~3

C) git reset --mixed HEAD~3

D) git checkout HEAD~3

Answer: C

Explanation: The git reset --mixed HEAD~3 command resets the last 3 commits but keeps the changes in the working directory, allowing you to modify them before recommitting.

566. Scenario: You are contributing to an open-source repository, and you need to find all the .py files that contain the word TODO.

Question: Which command will achieve this?

A) grep -r TODO *.py

B) grep TODO *.py

C) grep -r TODO --include=*.py

D) grep -i TODO *.py

Answer: C

Explanation: The grep -r TODO --include=*.py command recursively searches for the word TODO in all .py files, ensuring that only Python files are included in the search.

567. Scenario: You are debugging a Node.js application and want to inspect memory usage.

Question: Which command allows you to profile memory usage in a Node.js application?

A) node --inspect

B) node --trace-warnings

C) node --heap-prof

D) node --debug

Answer: C

Explanation: The node --heap-prof command generates a heap profile for memory usage in the Node.js application, which can be analyzed to debug memory leaks or inefficiencies.

568. Scenario: You are building a Python script and want to check for syntax errors without running the code.

Question: Which command should you use?

A) python script.py

B) python -m py_compile script.py

C) python -c script.py

D) python --check script.py

Answer: B

Explanation: The python -m py_compile script.py command checks the syntax of the script and compiles it into .pyc files without executing the code.

569. Scenario: You are contributing to an open-source project that uses Docker. You want to stop and remove all running containers.

Question: Which combination of commands achieves this?

A) docker kill $(docker ps -q) and docker rm $(docker ps -a -q)

B) docker stop $(docker ps -q) and docker rm -f $(docker ps -q)

C) docker stop $(docker ps -q) and docker rm $(docker ps -a -q)

D) docker down

Answer: C

Explanation: The docker stop $(docker ps -q) command stops all running containers, and docker rm $(docker ps -a -q) removes all stopped containers.

570. Scenario: You are learning Bash scripting and need to write a script that accepts a filename as input and prints the number of lines in the file.

Question: Which of the following Bash commands achieves this?

```
#!/bin/bash


_____

echo "The file contains $lines lines."
```

A) lines=$(wc -l $1 | cut -d' ' -f1)

B) lines=$(cat $1 | wc -l)

C) lines=$(wc -l < $1)

D) All of the above

Answer: D

Explanation: All the listed approaches correctly count the number of lines in a file. The wc -l command is the core utility used in all these methods.

571. Scenario: You are contributing to an open-source repository and need to check for unused imports in a Python file.

Question: Which command can help you identify unused imports?

A) pylint file.py

B) flake8 file.py

C) pycodestyle file.py

D) autopep8 file.py

Answer: A

Explanation: The pylint tool analyzes Python code and reports unused imports, along with other issues like unused variables and coding standard violations.

572. Scenario: You are building a React app and want to start the development server.

Question: Which command starts the React development server?

A) npm start

B) npm run

C) react start

D) npm build

Answer: A

Explanation: The npm start command starts the React development server, enabling you to test your application locally.

573. Scenario: You are contributing to an open-source project that uses Kubernetes, and you need to view the logs of a specific pod.

Question: Which command shows the logs of a pod named my-pod?

A) kubectl get logs my-pod

B) kubectl logs my-pod

C) kubectl describe logs my-pod

D) kubectl pod-logs my-pod

Answer: B

Explanation: The kubectl logs my-pod command retrieves and displays the logs of the specified Kubernetes pod, helping you debug its behavior.

574. Scenario: You are working on a Python project and want to create a virtual environment.

Question: Which command creates a virtual environment named env?

A) python -m venv env

B) python -m create env

C) python create venv env

D) python --virtual env

Answer: A

Explanation: The python -m venv env command creates a virtual environment in the env directory, isolating the project's dependencies.

575. Scenario: You are debugging a PostgreSQL database and need to list all tables in the current database.

Question: Which SQL command achieves this?

A) SHOW TABLES;

B) SELECT * FROM INFORMATION_SCHEMA.TABLES;

C) \dt

D) DESCRIBE TABLES;

Answer: C

Explanation: The \dt command in the PostgreSQL interactive terminal (psql) lists all tables in the current database schema.

576. Scenario: You are contributing to an open-source Python project and want to format a file according to PEP 8 standards.

Question: Which command reformats the file?

A) black file.py

B) pylint file.py --fix

C) autopep8 --in-place file.py

D) Both A and C

Answer: D

Explanation: Both black file.py and autopep8 --in-place file.py reformat the Python file according to PEP 8 standards, but black applies stricter formatting rules.

577. Scenario: You are learning JavaScript, and you need to destructure an object to extract its properties.

Question: Which code snippet correctly destructures the object?

const obj = { name: "John", age: 25 };

const { _____ } = obj;

A) name, age

B) obj.name, obj.age

C) name: obj.name, age: obj.age

D) name = obj.name, age = obj.age

Answer: A

Explanation: The syntax { name, age } correctly destructures the obj object, extracting its name and age properties into variables.

578. Scenario: You are debugging a Docker container and want to view its resource usage (CPU, memory).

Question: Which command shows this information?

A) docker stats

B) docker inspect

C) docker top

D) docker logs

Answer: A

Explanation: The docker stats command provides real-time resource usage statistics for running containers, including CPU and memory consumption.

579. Scenario: You want to check which processes are running inside a Docker container.

Question: Which command lists the processes in a container?

A) docker ps

B) docker top <container_id>

C) docker inspect <container_id>

D) docker logs <container_id>

Answer: B

Explanation: The docker top <container_id> command displays the processes running inside the specified container.

580. Scenario: You need to merge the feature branch into the main branch but want to ensure there are no merge conflicts beforehand.

Question: Which Git command should you use to check for conflicts without performing the merge?

A) git diff feature main

B) git merge --no-commit --no-ff feature

C) git merge --dry-run feature

D) git rebase --dry-run feature

Answer: C

Explanation: The git merge --dry-run feature command simulates the merge process without actually merging, allowing you to check for conflicts beforehand.

581. Scenario: You are working on a Linux machine and want to find the 5 largest files in your current directory.

Question: Which command will display this information?

A) du -ah | sort -rh | head -n 5

B) ls -lhS | head -n 5

C) find . -type f -exec du -h {} + | sort -rh | head -n 5

D) ls -l | sort -rh | head -n 5

Answer: A

Explanation: The du -ah command lists all files and directories with their sizes, which are then sorted in reverse order (sort -rh) and limited to 5 entries using head -n 5.

582. Scenario: You want to kill a process running on a specific port (e.g., port 8080) on Linux.

Question: Which combination of commands will achieve this?

A) lsof -i:8080; kill -9 <pid>

B) ps -aux | grep 8080; kill <pid>

C) netstat -tuln | grep 8080; kill <pid>

D) killall -9 8080

Answer: A

Explanation: The lsof -i:8080 command lists the process ID (PID) using port 8080, which can then be terminated with kill -9 <pid>.

583. Scenario: You need to create a compressed archive of a directory named project using the tar command.

Question: Which command will create a .tar.gz archive?

A) tar -cvf project.tar.gz project

B) tar -czvf project.tar.gz project

C) tar -cv project.tar.gz project

D) tar -cf project project.tar.gz

Answer: B

Explanation: The tar -czvf project.tar.gz project command creates a compressed (-z) archive (project.tar.gz) of the project directory with verbose output (-v).

584. Scenario: You are debugging a Kubernetes pod and need to execute a command inside the pod named web-app.

Question: Which command allows you to execute an interactive shell inside the pod?

A) kubectl exec web-app -- /bin/bash

B) kubectl exec -it web-app -- /bin/bash

C) kubectl run web-app -- /bin/bash

D) kubectl access web-app -- /bin/bash

Answer: B

Explanation: The kubectl exec -it web-app -- /bin/bash command opens an interactive shell inside the specified Kubernetes pod, enabling debugging or troubleshooting.

585. Scenario: You want to view the history of commands executed in your current Linux shell session.

Question: Which command lists the command history?

A) history

B) bash --history

C) cat ~/.bash_history

D) commands

Answer: A

Explanation: The history command displays the history of commands executed in the current shell session, along with their command numbers.

586. Scenario: You are contributing to an open-source Python project and want to create a requirements.txt file listing all installed dependencies.

Question: Which command generates the requirements.txt file?

A) pip freeze > requirements.txt

B) pip list > requirements.txt

C) pip install --list > requirements.txt

D) pip save > requirements.txt

Answer: A

Explanation: The pip freeze > requirements.txt command lists all installed Python packages and their versions, saving them into a requirements.txt file.

587. Scenario: You need to check the disk usage of the /var directory on a Linux system.

Question: Which command provides this information?

A) df -h /var

B) du -sh /var

C) ls -lh /var

D) find /var -disk

Answer: B

Explanation: The du -sh /var command displays the total disk usage of the /var directory in a human-readable format (-h).

588. Scenario: You want to rename a Git branch from dev to development.

Question: What is the correct sequence of commands?

A) git branch -m dev development

B) git rename dev development

C) git branch --rename dev development

D) git switch dev development

Answer: A

Explanation: The git branch -m dev development command renames the branch dev to development in both local and remote repositories.

589. Scenario: You are debugging a Docker container and need to view its environment variables.

Question: Which command displays the container's environment variables?

A) docker inspect <container_id>

B) docker exec <container_id> env

C) docker env <container_id>

D) Both A and B

Answer: D

Explanation: Both docker inspect <container_id> (detailed metadata) and docker exec <container_id> env (runtime variables) allow you to view environment variables of a Docker container.

590. Scenario: You are working on a Linux system and want to schedule a script to run every day at midnight using cron.

Question: Which command opens the crontab for editing?

A) crontab -e

B) cron -e

C) edit-cron

D) schedule -e

Answer: A

Explanation: The crontab -e command opens the crontab file for editing, allowing you to schedule tasks to run periodically.

591. Scenario: You are troubleshooting a network issue and want to check if port 80 is open on a remote server.

Question: Which command checks the availability of port 80?

A) telnet <server_ip> 80

B) ping <server_ip> --port 80

C) nc -zv <server_ip> 80

D) Both A and C

Answer: D

Explanation: Both telnet <server_ip> 80 and nc -zv <server_ip> 80 check the availability of port 80 on the remote server. nc (netcat) is faster and more modern.

592. Scenario: You want to compress multiple .log files into a single .zip archive.

Question: Which command achieves this?

A) zip logs.zip *.log

B) tar -czvf logs.zip *.log

C) gzip *.log > logs.zip

D) compress *.log logs.zip

Answer: A

Explanation: The zip logs.zip *.log command compresses all .log files into a single archive named logs.zip.

593. Scenario: You are debugging a Linux server and want to display all currently open network connections.

Question: Which command provides this information?

A) netstat -tuln

B) lsof -i

C) ss -tuln

D) All of the above

Answer: D

Explanation: All listed commands (netstat, lsof, ss) display open network connections, with ss being the fastest and most modern tool.

www.ingramcontent.com/pod-product-compliance
Lightning Source LLC
Chambersburg PA
CBHW071413050326
40689CB00010B/1850